Soap That Doesn't Clean

Soap That Doesn't Clean

Tyrone Garcia

iUniverse, Inc.
Bloomington

SOAP THAT DOESN'T CLEAN

iUniverse books may be ordered through booksellers or by contacting:

iUniverse
1663 Liberty Drive
Bloomington, IN 47403
www.iuniverse.com
1-800-Authors (1-800-288-4677)

ISBN: 978-1-4759-7950-3 (sc)
ISBN: 978-1-4759-7951-0 (ebk)

Library of Congress Control Number: 2013903735

Printed in the United States of America

iUniverse rev. date: 03/21/2013

I want to dedicate this book to all the people who fought and never gave up. For all the people who have been stepped on, but kept their heads up, and all the people who died on the streets from drugs, alcohol, and gang violence including my friend Augustine Rodriquez, My brother Angelo Garcia, My family who stood by my side always and to my beloved wife Teresita Garcia. An addition To Eliacil Reyes Garcia, Leonides Vargas Cruz, Ana Vargas Acosta, and Angelina Vasquez Garcia. My parents and my kids Andre's leonell, Jeanette, Jackie, and Sonia, and the two newest members little baby Rios, and baby Angelina.

Introduction

As I stood in front of the class full of white kids, I felt as my world had come to an end. They were laughing at me for I was forced to sit in garbage pail that was full of crushed up art paper. When I was given permission to get up a piece of art paper was stuck to my backside. The class thought I looked funny. Then the nun said that I was worthless. She gave me the impression of being an outcast. Outcast I would become. I went home and tried to clean the dark skin of my body for I hated who I was. Society had labeled Puerto Ricans as car thieves, welfare recipient, and a menace to their "civilized" society. I was only a child, but I was Puerto Rican. I was learning about hate and prejudice during my path of self discovery.

I wrote this book to prove that just because you have chosen a bad road doesn't mean you can't change, however; you can't change who you are neither. How an individual can be impacted by the ignorance and wrong doings of a person when young. What happened to me in the first grade impacted me till the age of 30; I would live in anger and hated a race of people for the actions of several. My mother's respect for the church blinded her from the mistreatment I was receiving from the nuns who abused me mentally and physically. Corporal punishment just brought out the anger in me, because I couldn't protect myself, and when I did it wasn't the correct way.

In 1987 I was thinking of writing a book when I came out of my first rehab drug and alcohol abuse, It took until May 2012, for me to write. While sending an email to Professor Ginette Eldredge, who was teaching me Spanish at the time. I saw a poem on the bottom of her email. I meditated on it for several months than later I found out it was the last words of Segismundo Soliliquay, The son of a 14 century king in Poland. His father the king was told that his son could never rule as king, because he was going to be a bad one. The Father took the advice and locked him up in a tower. As time went on the king came to the conclusion that his son Segismundo should be allowed to be the king when it was his time. He would then become king and just as the people advised the dad he was a terrible and violent king. Eventually he was drugged and sent back to the tower and slept. When he awakened he said he had a bad dream and that he didn't like what he dreamed about. The guards told him yes! He was dreaming. He then changed his life around even though he lost his kingdom he decided to live more righteous

I believe my life was almost the same in a different time and certainly not the son of a king. However I did live violently and not only hurt myself I hurt others. While in rehab I did wake up the next day a different man and was able to make big changes in my life. So I feel I need to share with others of my failures and success. This book is for People who are victims of discrimination, people who have low self esteem, People who were abused mentally when young, and people who were told they wouldn't amount to anything. People struggling from addiction, bad business decisions, people who in general have no fight in them, people who had lost everything in a bad business venture and see themselves left with no more resources, people who need to climb out of the abyss of constant problems and need faith to deal with it. Allowing the Supreme Being to do for you what you cannot do for yourself. And doing the things you can do for yourself.

There are so many different scenarios in my life that all people can relate to. From racism, gang life, inner city life, violence, to a world traveler on a ship and getting sober and becoming a Business man in middle class America, living the suburban life. It's like my life was put through so many obstacles in order for me to write this book. I feel the book will help many people, and provide them hope for a better future and to look at life more like an education not an omen.

Chapter 1

Hey man let me borrow twenty dollars I will pay you on Friday. Walking the streets late at night looking for that high, that high I will never feel again, lying to the people so I can get a hit of some crack and maybe a sip of beer. Wow that chick over there looks so good! maybe a dime bag will get me laid. Let me see what I can steal so I could sell it. "Boy" do I feel sick to my mind and sick of getting high, but how do I escape the inescapable? Oh shit run! Tyrone someone is shooting at you run Tyrone run.

That's just the way it was for many years until I woke up and started to learn the truth about myself. Let me tell you how it happened. My name is Tyrone Joseph Garcia. I was born on Thursday, February 9th 1961 at 11: 15 am in Jacobi Hospital, which is located in the boogie down Bronx, New York. However, my spirit came from Puerto Rico. I was born in the decade of the assassinations of John F Kennedy, Robert F Kennedy, Malcolm X, Martin Luther King, and one of my personal heroes, Dr. Pedro Albizo Campos. Although Campos wasn't assassinated as the media would have wanted you to know. He was killed slowly and tortured in an Atlanta Federal Prison and also in Puerto Rico, like many others, who had something good to bring to this world. All fought for the freedom of civil rights, and the right to live. The sixties was a time of racism, war in Viet Nam, the poor being drafted and the rich hiding their sons by sending them to college. Puerto Ricans, who weren't able to vote for the President in Puerto Rico, were also drafted and sent to war. Everything went wrong in the 60s; racism played a big role in America. There was war in our very own streets over the war in Viet Nam, and heroin was leading the way. A lot of black leaders and several Puerto Rican leaders were killed or tortured, hate was the new order and I was born right in the middle of it.

I was named Tyrone, because my mother liked Tyrone Power the actor. The name Tyrone comes from a small town in Ireland, how confused was my mom! As a little Puerto Rican lad, I was always asked the question how did I get the name Tyrone? I would answer, my mom loved Tyrone Power, the actor and leave it at that. I never did like my name. I would have preferred Julio over Tyrone anytime. It could have been worse! they could of called me Jesus. The Cuban Missile crises, was another problem at that time, I was 1 years old thank God! America had the right Man in the white house JFK. Imagine some crackpot gung ho politician in charge. We all would be glowing in the dark. That was 1962. Martin Luther King brought us rights we did not have, respect", we got some, but it was Malcolm X that brought fear to America. While King taught us to turn the other cheek, Malcolm X said if they hit you hit them right back.

My favorite leader is Dr. Pedro Albizzu Campos. He was the Malcolm X of Puerto Rico. He fought for Puerto Rico's Independence from The US. However U.S. officials and traitor Puerto Ricans went against him in order for the US to stay in control of Puerto Rico, only to throw it in our faces for the rest of our lives. Puerto Rico, at one time was a paradise for the original people, the Tiano people. In 1492 Columbus, while lost at sea, came across the Caribbean Island of Guanahanii which is Tiano for Las Bahamas. Spain would conquer and become the new owners of the Island, Who are they? Well History tells us that the moors enslaved Spain. So how many races are involved here? They also brought African Slaves, oh God! who the hell am I? As the new Spanish regime swallowed up South, central, and some parts of North America, all indigenous people were murdered or enslaved into the new way of life Christianity, and Spanish rule. That would last until 1898 When the US in a fair fight, I guess! Dethroned Spain, In 1897 Spain had already given full autonomy to Puerto Rico to be independent. By the time Puerto Rico was finish building their new government, US soldiers came marching through Ponce. The islands resources were a big asset for the US, Bananas, coffee, gold, or what was left of the gold, tobacco, vegetables galore, and of course free labor. By 1917 Puerto Ricans were US citizens. Then he we go to WW 1, Dr. Pedro Albizu Campos was an Officer in that war he served in an African American regiment. Then after the war went to Harvard and became a lawyer and the leader of the Puerto Rican Nationalist party. His only complain was? How can America take over a country legally without governmental consent? Puerto Rico was a sovereign independent country under international law already with a working government.

I think it's a shame that many Puerto Ricans don't know who this man was. But I will get back to this later in my story.

When I was 2 years old I went to Puerto Rico and for some reason I always remember looking out the window of the plane and watching the sun shine upon my face. I felt peace as I believe I was very still my mother tells me. I remember when we arrived in Puerto Rico, I saw a house made of wood it was my Aunt Celia house and uncle Cheo. I don't know how I remember, but for some reason I do. He had roosters and you could hear them in the morning. I also believed he had pigs, because when I use to ask my mom later on in my life how they were? I would say, ¿ *cómo estan los Puercos de cheo? "How are cheos pigs doing"*.

I started school in 1967 where I went to kindergarten, I was 6 years old. I started the 1st grade in a private school. My sister Maritza and brother Jimmy were already there and were ahead of me, I was the youngest of a family of 4 boys and 1 girl, Jose, Angelo RIP, Jimmy, Maritza, and me, and I can't leave out Twila, Twila was the daughter of my cousin Opi, but was with us for a long while so she was like our little sister.

My first teacher was a nun she treated everyone bad, but for some reason she treated me worse. In those days corporal punishment was accepted in the schools system and in the home. That nun put so much fear in me I would be afraid to ask her anything. When I did ask, she would tell me no. I would be scared to ask any questions, for fear of sounding dumb. That made learning hard for me throughout my academic career I would lack confidence. I was always afraid to ask the teacher, so most of my learning experience was guessing for the right answer. She taught with anger and would slap me in my face constantly. It would become part of the curriculum, in other punishments; we were told to bend over and get wacked with a long stick against our butts. It was becoming amusing to us for we didn't know any better.

One day and it's still humiliating for me to replay this, but on one occasion I urinated on myself which created a puddle on the floor. I wasn't allowed to go to the bathroom so I would urinate on myself from trying to hold it. She got very mad and hit me several times. She told me to rub my nose in it like you would do a dog. I said no, but she would hit me and hit me until I decided to rub my face in it like a dog, after, she told me to sit in a garbage pail in front of the class. She said I was worthless. I just sat there satisfied that she wasn't hitting me anymore, but very angry. When I got up a piece of paper from the garbage was glued to my butt, as I walked I looked like an animal and everybody laughed at me, it was a very bad day for me, I was 7 years old. I would go home that day, and I was trying to clean the dark skin of my body, you see all the kids were white so since I was different I started to believe that maybe if a cleaned off the dark skin. I would be accepted. I would get left back in the first grade, what a start to a life that would have obstacle after obstacle ahead.

I was an altar boy at St Joan of Arc parish, Fr Salamini, was the Parrish priest. He was a great one. I told him what had happen and he went over to the school and complained and really was angry over it. My mother was a catholic when I told her about what the nun was doing to me; she didn't want to believe me. Fr Salimini took care of the matter and the nun backed off a little. He told me to come to him whenever I was in trouble. I felt like God sent him to protect me.

The damage was done anything white was my enemy the 60s had affected me just like everybody else, a character defect I would inherit from those people. I was not born with hate or racism I was introduced into it. We would go back and forth spic, nigger, honkie, mic, Wap, Out of all the races, I respected Italians, even though they called us spics to, I always looked at them as equals because some of them were dark to, being part Spanish, puts me in the real Latin circle France, Portugal, Spain, and Italy, for what I've learned. Fr. Salamini, was Italian and he was a true priest and great person. On Fridays we would go to alter boy meetings to get the Sunday schedule and then play football or baseball in the church parking lot. I loved Fr. Salamini allot he was fun and he understood the pressure us kids were under living in the hood. I remember wearing my gang colors while wearing our black and white altar boy clothes. I than quit because, I was ashamed of serving mass and being in a gang, I had to choose, my heart wanted the church my anger wanted the gang. When I quit I remember Fr. Salamini looking sad and saying "you're quitting on me" I understand".

I would became an animal of the worse kind, by the time I was in the 4ʳᵈ grade I was involved in a gang they were called satins angels, "what the hell" I always believe when you do something do it right. Gangs were a group of angry kids with attitudes looking for trouble and looking for friendship. We were from ages 10 to 15 and some older. Being part of a crew meant something, it got you respect and it was also a lot of fun, you learned everything in the streets, sex, was one, when I learned that you had to have sex in order to have kids I freaked out because I could never see my mom and dad do that. I got into a fight with the kid who told me. When we were young learning in the streets we would look at pornographic sex so you would think it was just a practice for sexy people and wild woman. I couldn't see my mom do those things so I just thought my friend was joking with me. That night I asked my mom if she had sex with my dad in order to have me, when I thought it was God who sent me, my dad walks away laughing and my Dramatic mom makes a show and says "it's the sin we had to do in order to bring you into this world that's why we suffer when we have you." Great answer mom" but it's called reproducing, there would be better days.

My Farther started The Bronx River Spanish club, it had almost 50 members, with the kids we were almost 200 people. We would do *parandas* at Christmas in the building. *Parandas* is part of the Puerto Rican culture, what we would do is start with a little group with instruments or whatever made noise and sing, knock on someone door, and go into their house and party. They would have to feed us something and pass on the alcohol. It was my first encounter with alcohol. When my parents were not looking, I would take a shot of *coquito*, a Puerto Rican drink made with coconut and rum . . . Then they would join us and we would go to another house until 5 in the morning. That was fun. My dad would also put together *la jiras* 4 to 5 busses full of Puerto Ricans, we would go to upstate NY were there were beautiful lakes and parks. The Mondays before the trip I was happy, because it was a lot of fun most of the neighborhood would go, the trip would be on Saturdays so all week I was waiting for Saturday along with my friends.

Community life was so segregated back then, but we lived together, PR with PR, Blacks with Blacks, whites with whites, when the summer was over it meant back to the Insane Asylum called school. Fear would fill my body because I had to deal with much racism. Before my 3ʳᵈ year of school was over another nun tried to hit me. I grabbed her hand and I said" no you are not going to hit me anymore" I was sick and tired of the abuse, and I started fighting back in order to protect myself. I would try to participate in class, but I would be ridiculed, because since I was always afraid to ask questions about what we were learning. I would sound dumb. I would just try to figure it out. I was terrible in school I was a 65-70 student, when the other students got 85 and 90s I would just say to myself that they are white they are smarter than me. I believe God gave me the answers at certain times when I was taking test, because I didn't know much of anything. I would just pray and ask God to give me the answers. I would fight and argue constantly with others and over race, I felt very lonely so for most of the time I would just be to myself, but I would always daydream about good things that I would love to have and would write and draw pictures in class. I would draw a ship and a house.

My gang life was also growing and I was on my way towards a terrible life. The fifth grade was a little better we were getting more teachers than nuns and they did treat us better. There was another student who was Puerto Rican his name was Patrick, we hung out together, and I felt a little better now that I had another PR with me, but he was very bad and was kicked out of school by the end of the year. The school did a lot of shows that would involve the students, I was in all of them, because I was good at dancing and singing with the other students, and though I was dark, I was a very good looking young man. Than by the 7th grade I was more accepted, because I was good in basketball, Baseball, football, and track & field, things started to change, but my heart was so full of anger and my gang life was still growing. I met night owl a friend we were in a gang called the Supreme Enchanters, but in a younger division, I was the war council, he was the president. I remember One time I was jumped after school by some white boys and I ran to the clubhouse of my gang and told night owl. The next day there were about 50 Puerto Ricans, from my gang outside the school waiting to protect me from anybody who threatened me. Farther D, the school priest comes up to my class with spike next to him another member spike who was wearing a chain across his body, I had the whole school worried. I was asked to tell them to go home because it was creating a panic. I told FR.D what had happen and they were only here for my protection. He pleaded with me for them to leave. I looked at him and said ok. I have to admit it felt great and I noticed that power was needed in order to get respect. The 8th and final grade of that dreadful school would come and there were more Puerto Ricans about 5-6, I graduated in 1976 in the Bicentennial year and never looked back. Our graduation song was, we only just begun" by the carpenters, Thanks" what lies ahead.

I pass my co-op test to qualify for catholic HS, St Helena commercial. I told my dad I rather go to public HS. What I did not know was that 1976 would be my last real year of actually attending classes. The High School I went to was 2 blocks from my house it was mostly black and Puerto Rican. The staircases had cages built around it and there were Police, plus heavy security. You had the several street gangs. I felt right at home remember" I was an animal. When I attended my first class, It was different just people sitting in the classroom talking and doing what they wanted. My best class was Mr. Goodman he actually was an exciting teacher who cared, he jump on his table and act out his history lesson, eventually I would stop going to class. I was drinking and smoking pot. It's funny how someone's character defects could have such a great impact on someone's life. I would enjoy getting high and chasing girls, but I was very shy with the woman. I always had trouble asking, I always had fear of rejection. My first girlfriend took me over 3 hours to ask her to be my girl, her name was Nydia. Nite owl had to confirm to me many times that she liked me. When I asked her, I said "do you want to be my girl" very slowly and very low, after generating all that courage she says what? I turned red like a tomato and said it again and she said yes. I was very happy. Though I was a very angry man I always respected woman I never put my hands on one in a bad way. My mother and farther loved each other and my dad was a real gentleman.

Alcohol, and drugs, was starting to take over me. I worked to support my habit and buy the latest clothes so I would look good. I wanted to move up the ranks in my gang, so I had to fight this guy; I did and almost beat him. I was giving respect by the gang. My older brother Jose was also a gang member in earlier years. He was the president of the reapers in our neighborhood. He wasn't a bad guy he loved talking politics and was very smart he was the oldest. I was given respect, because of Jose my brother. My second oldest brother Angelo was not involved in street gangs; he was more of a white collar criminal who wore suits. He would be the first to die from the family. Angelo being my brother also earned me respect for his associates was pretty tough. Nobody messed with me, because my family was like a little mafia. My poor dad who came from Puerto Rico for a better life, who was a hard honest working class man must of felt down his kids were becoming loosers. My brother Jimmy was all pro High School Football player He was accepted to many good football colleges, my dad was very proud of him, but on an unfortunate night he hurt his leg bad and couldn't play.

The majority of my cousins In PR on my dads side were educated with college degrees, Manolo, Mildread, Anita, victor, 2 of them has doctrines. And not to leave out Opi, and Tony, So our genes were good it was our atmosphere that wasn't. Don't worry Dad your youngest will surprise you one day. New York was a real hell hole for many PRs, but not all a lot of PRs also found success in the US I would say very little. Me and niteowl recruited some guys from tremont ave. They wanted protection so we made another division of enchanters that would bring us more money, however we had to kick money to the leaders which was ceasar and Harry.

New York had its reputation of being a gangster town, they made many movies about them James Cagney who was an actor played the role of one of my favorate gangsters the movie, "Angels with dirty faces" was one of my best movies which Cagney started in. A lot of us ghetto kids saw that was the only capitolism available to us. "The Godfather" was the best Gangster

Film of all times in my book, Marlon Brando started it but Al Pacino ended it; and I would become a fan of him.

Bronx River had 3 areas were you would hangout during the day. The basketball courts mostly blacks, the handball court Puerto Rican, and at the end of the day you hung out in the circle by the community center were they had benches and tables. My older brother Jose and his friend Stevie, David, Manny, Richie, Charley, would hang out and discussed politics. They were working on changing the country with their dialogue; that would turn into screaming arguments between Stevie, and David, most of the time. I would hang out with them for a while but then leave, I hung with Mousy in front of the park where he would gamble and play dice 7/11 or 3 dice, the problem with Mousy was he would win, but his addictive behavior to continue playing would lose his winnings. His girlfriend Lizzie would spend hours waiting for him and sometimes we all were going some were, but it would be 11 pm and he was still gambling so we just talk and hangout.

At night the Puerto Ricans were playing with their congas, timbales, and playing music, and the projects at night sounded like Puerto Rico in the beginning when the African drum would sound off in the jungle. We would sing and have a great time. Most nights all was calm we were just following our heritage and culture which was playing music and having some fun. We all got along fine and there was respect amongst us. Drugs though were not part of our culture it was part of the American social order, and if you was living in America they was a good chance you experienced smoking pot or using all other types of illegal drugs. Drugs didn't grow in Harlem or the South Bronx it grew in South America, Europe, Asia; ETC. Somebody had to bring it in to the country some way. Drugs were allowed in the bad neighborhoods the cops wouldn't do much to stop it. They figure as long as it stayed in the Black and Latino sections of town all would be good. Drugs were a weapon of mass destruction.

One night we had a problem with another gang The Dragons, we marched all the way down Tremont Avenue to deal with them. I was pretty worried, but since some of us had weapons, I wasn't worry, me myself I had my hands like always. When we got there, Nitman, and Taste, went in to talk and we stood outside. An hour went by and all the members left, but nitman, and taste, was still inside. I stood with another gang member alone outside, for another hour or so and they would not come out, Joey looks at me and says "let's go" "there is nothing we could do". I felt as we left behind 2 of our partners, I was scared. The guys with the weapons had left. I was only 16 at the time. Nitman, and taste, became part of the dragons, they were both pissed! but my question is? Why didn't they come out and say all was fine. I mean they never did! I at one time felt they were dead. Nitman, would feel betrayed at all of us eventually and go his own way.

The gangs were gone by 1977 they were small crews, my crew would be Mousy, Felix, and harry, we had a car, or it was Mousy's car A 71 Ford Marquis. We hung out and had a lot of fun going to parties. We would get high and party all night, drinking beer and driving in a car not worrying about the police. DUI's should have been given, but in that area the police just build their perimeter and made sure we didn't pass it. I had a lot of fun times with my crew, we did some funny things and would meet allot of woman. Dancing Salsa, freestyle, or break dancing were the style back then. The hairstyle was either an Afro or DA. The DA was the hair style Jon Travolta had in the Movie "Saturday Night Fever". I had an afro and wore a dashiki I remember my aunt visiting from Puerto Rico when I arrived at my home she was there and when she sees me she says "Who's That" I looked like a ghetto man with an attitude. For me I felt righteous. "Right on" "Power to the People" "groovy Man" "What's up papa". "That's tight" "pass the joint bro" or "Que pasa bro" "tu nosabe nada" "hey mira" "dame una soda". These were the words we spoke when communicating with each other. The words meant something, it was called street slang. For some of us Puerto Ricans It was destroying the Spanish language along with the English one.

I got my first Job in 1978 it was a program with the city of N.Y. for H.S. dropouts it paid us about $ 400.00 every 2 weeks. I met some brothers from, Bronxdale Projects, Sterling, Clem, Eddie, Yan, Gary, Cowboy, all worked at the same place. Bronxdale was home of the Black Spades along with Bronx River, where I lived. The Black Spades were one of the biggest Gangs in all NYC mostly Black members, but many Puerto Ricans were also involved. However at that time they were mostly small crews like us, Street gangs were pretty dead. The organization was the new name. Every time we got paid we would go to the stores and buy clothes, and go to 42nd street Manhattan, walk around try to meet girls or go to see karate movies. The job duties we did were, paint, cut grass, and train so we could get a Job, and get our GED. None of us did! Get our GED for what I know. The program was eventually cut, but some of the guys when they became 18 years old were able to get jobs with City Housing, so it was positive. Jimmy Carter was the president at the time and he created budgets for these urban city programs that did help some. It Help several of us. For me I was learning how not to budget money. I would be broke within hours of getting paid. Money for me would always go quick, it never last. We cleaned up allot of the neighborhood and I also asked my boss to let us clean up the Local Church and paint their fence.

I remember DJ Africa Bambaataa, who was a great DJ at the time. He lived on the first floor and he would put his speakers outside his window and DJ. We would stand around and listen and have a great time with his Djaying. The Zulu Nation was born In Bronx River and a lot of them were tough gang kids converted into a group of very talented young break dancers, in Bronx River. The movement became very positive for many young Black and Latinos.,

Bambaataa was very Educated he did not use any drugs or drank alcohol he was a true person when coming down to his beliefs and gave many great parties and bought culture to everyone who wanted it. I am grateful for being part of that growth in Bronx River, he is still in the music business. As for what happen to the Black Spades? Today they do a lot of community service and are trying to reach the community and find solutions to their problems; Amber being one of them is one of the biggest volunteers involved and always trying to help her fellow human. I would say both are strong leaders in the community.

We had a Community Center in Bronx River, in the back, there was a stage and Bambaataa would perform there with his DJ equipment and we would party till 12-1am, or until the police come tell us to turn off the music. It was fun and we all would break dance whenever he played certain songs. Though I was not a premiere dancer in that form, I tried.

Alcohol continued to be my medicine for socializing. I was very shy but when I drank I wasn't afraid to do anything that came to my mind. I one time just for the hell of it punched some poor guy in the face at a party. He was too scared to hit me back because he was in Bronx River; my neighborhood had developed a reputation for being one of the worse projects in the Bronx. People would be scared when they came over to hear music in Bronx River. One night Bam was performing at a location in Yonkers New York, I and Gary were playing taxi. We were picking up and dropping off charging 5.00 a head. On our way back there was car in the middle of the highway. I don't know, but Gary was able to turn hard and miss hitting that car, we would have all been dead, because no one had seatbelts on. I would have flown right out the window. After; I noticed that I was saved by something. I always believed in God, but we were brought up to believe in a punishing God who would than later love you "how contradicting".

1977 was also the year I met a girl from Jamaica, she lived in Canada, but was in Bronx River visiting family for the summer. We got along fine, and she became my girl. It was the first time I had real intimate relations with a woman. I was 16 years old. She was a beautiful black woman, and I enjoyed being with her that summer. She would come back the following summer with a child, but told me it wasn't mine. I looked at the child and he looked like me, but I did not pursue it, so I will never know, I couldn't do anything anyway I was 16. However if it was mine, I would of done something.

My parents moved to Bronx River in 1956, when the projects were still pretty new. My father's name was Eliacil Garcia Reyes, My mother was Angelina Vasquez Garcia, and they were married in 1952. My dad had a great opportunity in Puerto Rico, but decided to come to America. I sometimes wish he would have stood in Puerto Rico, but then I wouldn't know the people I know today, so it balances out. In 1969-70 MY Dad was a great help with the campaign of Herman Badillo the first Puerto Rican to run for mayor of the city of N.Y. He would lose to Abraham Beame, but" not by much. Puerto Ricans were not getting a fair share of the summer jobs that were available for teenage kids. Blacks were stronger than us in the projects. My Dad was a big community leader along with Miss Hoard, and others, The Delgado family in apartment 11-f Ramon and Gloria Delgado were the other family, Garcia-Delgado were the foundation of Puerto Ricans in 1440. The Delgado's would have great parties and Ramon made the best devil eggs and Ham in the world. There were also other families in the building like Lolita, Judy, Sarah, Bonilla, Johnny, Lucy and Ricky, and so many more. We were all family and if one of them caught you doing something wrong they would stop you and tell your parents. Friends were real and so were families. It may have been low income but our culture was high and pride was big. Everybody was catholic so every month there was a party. Confirmation, Communion, Baptism, Christmas, thanksgiving, whatever! There was always a gathering of all the families and La Fiesta begins. How I would love to relive those days of happiness and glory. For we never had many problems until some of us started using drugs.

My sister Maritza was about the only good child at home. I am very close to her, when my mother had to go out, she would take care of me and play this stupid scary game called El Hombre" the man, I would get scared and she would get her thrills, but one day she did it so good, that she scared herself, and we both were hiding in the closet waiting for our mother. Back in those days you were always getting hit either by the teacher or your parents. I do agree It made us stronger, but it affected me different. My other brother Jimmy was completely different he went to my same school and got along with the white boys so good that after he Graduated from James Monroe High School he went back to Parkchester and moved in with them. My sister also graduated from James Monroe High School, But like my other 2 older brothers Jose and Angelo I did not. I never even participated at Monroe. Many people did graduate from the school, for me everything looked different. I guess that awful day in my 1st grade class humiliated me so much. I still today when I think about it I feel embarrassed talking or thinking about it. Low self esteem is what clouded my inner self for many years. My negative feelings damage any enthused feeling I may get; for success wasn't in my future. Getting by is all I care about. I would go through my teenage life playing the fool, who needs to be laughed at in order to get attention or accepted. When dinking and a song I liked come on, I dance crazy they would say "go Tyrone go "Making other people laugh, will be me goal.

The first time I went to jail I remember I was carrying a switch blade. A cop saw it in my back pocket and arrested me. My first reaction was my mother how will she take it? I would also feel good, because I have experienced being locked up. How ignorant are we in the hood" Sleeping on a hard piece of wood is not that Cool, then eating terrible sandwiches and cold coffee. I was put in handcuffs along with several others. I would ride the famous paddy wagon and felt as my hero James Cagney. Then to 100 Centre Street Criminal Court I go. There I would be put in a large cell full of other criminals. I was not as comfortable as I thought I would be! The toilet in the cell was visible for all can see. How can I take a dump in front of so many people? I was giving 6 mounts probation for having a weapon, me being 16, meant it would be thrown out later.

1979, my crew decided to become a loyal to each other in business. We put some money together and decided to make more money together. New York. was a funny city, it did not care about black and Puerto Rican neighborhoods, one time they was an investigation for a crime and detectives were asking questions in the park while others sold pot there. I mean it was just like owning a candy store, as long as you showed them some respect they didn't care "kill yourselves "niggers and spics" It's like society wanted us to commit those types of crimes, as long as it stood in the neighborhood its ok. I guess they had to justify calling us animals when watching the news.

One night when partying in the center Harry decided to sucker punch the wrong guy; he was a part of group and a long time family member of Bronx River. The man was scared, but had Harry in a head lock, while we were trying to stop it a man, was holding a gun at us asking his friend, weather to shoot at us or not. The Friend, who was also our friend and knew my family told him no, but was pissed that Harry did that. It was the first time I saw a gun in my face that close. I did pass the test, I did not run and leave my friends, I was scared, but I accepted death because that was the only guarantee in our lives. When you belong to a crew you live and die with your decisions nothing else is accepted. We left and the next day all was well. There would be another time it would be at ward and Watson.

We continue to make money and like always one of the group members have to be greedy Harry, and his girl took control of the money and they spend the money on themselves. From the crew I and Atone were the youngest and the closes. We went back to my first gang Satins Angels and the baby Spades. I did not last long with the baby spades, because my brother spent a lot of time with the Black Spades and did not want to see me involved, so I couldn't go to the meetings in the old center. Clifford was the pres. And Kevin, was the vice pres. it didn't matter, In Bronx River almost everybody was a Black Spade, or Reaper, at that time.

Hanging out with your gang to the wee hours of the morning was part of growing up. You were afraid you miss something if you went home early. In June or July I would get busted and locked up again. We were driving around listening to music and smoking pot. The police pulled us over a rare thing but, I believe we were being watched. The cop searched the car and found a ½ ounce of pot. My friend Harry had a record and on parole. I decided to take the rap for the drugs in order for him not to go back to Jail for a longer term. I was handcuffed and put in the police car and taken to Jail, I was dedicated to my crew and would do anything to make sure my word meant something. I was 18 which meant I was of adult age and it could be serious. But, it was dropped down to a disorderly conduct. In NY you really had to have a lot of drugs on you to be taken serious. While walking back to the Projects from Jail I looked at my surroundings and from block to block meditated on what my life was and what would be my ending. It was an experience for me who was going 100 miles an hour. I was able to think about what I was doing and acknowledging that my only way out would be death.

That same year Iran took over the embassy in Tehran We were just 4 years after that crazy Viet Nam war and we thought we were going into another, Jimmy Carter was President and he asked that all 18 year old sign up for the selective service. I was hoping to go fight because inside I really wanted to leave the life I was living, it was starting to get to me. I remember one time sitting in front of 7 to midnight, a store in the neighborhood, I was smoking pot and I said to myself is this going to be my life, This housing projects, I tried to join the army but I did not have a High School Diploma so I couldn't. I was feeling like I was in a prison without the possibility of parole.

Chapter 2

In 1980, Ronald Reagan, became President of the United States. Allot of programs that were helping the poor were cut and poverty got worse, selling drugs was becoming very attractive for people who were struggling financially especially the ones using it. Drugs started taking over the streets and people couldn't do anything about it. I was told by someone that in the National Guard you didn't need a High School diploma and if you missed your weekend drills you were ordered to active duty. It would happen to my Brother Jose, mousy, and several others. So I joined and went to boot camp at FT Sill Oklahoma, for 8 weeks. New York was going crazy and I was trying to escape. My drug addiction was getting worse and I was becoming a bum at a very young age.

When I landed in Lawton Oklahoma, I would experience a different way of life. I saw allot of country people and allot of Indians. The weather was cold in the morning and hot in the middle of the day it was March 1980. It felt like I was in another world. I would feel free from the ghetto. I would meet my Drill Instructor, Like I expected allot of yelling, and tough talking, I fitted right in, loved it" real fighting words to turn me into a soldier. We were always being punished and pushups were what we had to do. "Get down and give me 20" was the way they told you to do pushups. We run every morning and sing cadence "Mama and papa were lying in bed, mama rolled over and papa said I want to be an airborne ranger" and on it went. I really enjoyed army life for the little time I was there. I figure if I'm going to be a warrior and get killed it would be better if my family get's a check and a glory flag, instead of a bunch of gang members saying 'boy he was really cool'. When I was introduced into the M-16 A1 rifle I said Yeh buddy!!! I would love to have this in a gang war, you could take out a bunch of people with a 30 round banana clip in automatic mode.

One time while sitting outside myself and another soldier from Detroit, we were looking at the snack bar which was across the field from the barracks we were staying. We decided to throw on our work shirts and hat and very carefully walk over and get a couple pitchers of beer. We drank it and got back without getting in any trouble. I took allot of chances in my life, but that was really bold of me. I went though Boot Camp like the perfect student. I had no attitude I did everything they told me to do, and I studied what I needed to learn. As the weeks went by I started learning about being a soldier and what it meant. I wanted to stay there I didn't want to leave. In our last week I pass all that was required. I would of gotten a 100, but I forgot to put the safety on the M-60 machine gun, however, I was a Go, and not a No-Go which is how they scored you.

We were giving a pass to go into town and all there was were strips of bars with Hookers right outside the base, I do believe there were better places but when asking where was the hot spot that's where they sent us. Soldiers and Sailor's never go to nice places when on liberty alcohol and chicks is what most of us follow. I did not trust the area so I just kept is simple. I drank some beer and forced myself to go back to the base. The next day I went to see my platoon Sergeant, and I asked him how could I stay here in the army without having to go back to New York?, he told me he can't help me with that, after AIT [advance Individual training] I should ask my National Guard unit. I said ok. But I said it with sadness.

I went to Ft lee Virginia to Quartermaster School Motor pool & parts. Life is weird! I was in a state I would live within another decade, at least some 70 miles east from there. The training was all class room. I didn't do well, but I tried. I was giving more freedom to go into town so like a good soldier I met a girl there. We would go to the movies and mall, but it didn't work out so I just did my time there and drank with the fella's.

One day I got drunk and when I walked into the barracks the soldier on watch told me to take off my hat. I got mad and punched him right in the face; we fought and he got some good hits on me and me on him and they broke it up. I would get an article 14 which was 2 weeks suspension without pay; however I was National Guard and that will be assessed when I got back to New York. I did do some KP and peel potatoes and for me it wasn't a punishment cooking was one of my talents. I would learn about that trait later on in my life. I had a conversation with the Sergeant; he said I could've of gotten jail time, in war time maybe even shot. I struggled to pass the course so I was sent to Augusta Georgia FT Gordon, signalman school, field wireman. I was going to hook up communications in combat situations. So I was taught to run wire, hook up phones, switchboards and climb poles in order to fix and splice wire. I did that pretty good and I pass that class. I would prepare to leave, but before I left there was a wild night ahead with the crew, and the sergeants.

The sergeants and crew decided to have a party. We bought a lot of beer and we all got drunk. The sergeants beat up one of the recruits and another recruit was so drunk he decided to slam his arm into a glass wall and ripped his arm apart everything just went ballistic. I was a little worried, because it was our leaders who started it, 2 white sergeants for no apparent reason started beating on this black guy. I have seen this before and I said" wow" you just can't shake racism can you. It's very sad, even when honoring your country racial people within still have to mess up your glory. Even as a volunteer willing to fight for the rights of the American people. How can America weed these people out of circulation? I got my paperwork and went back to the boogie down Bronx. I reported for duty at the Franklyn Armory, on Boston Road, in The Bronx, The Rainbow Division 42 infantry Field Artillery. What a joke when I asked for my field gear I was told I had to earn it, something they were suppose to give me. The job of the Guard is to work for the State, in case of an emergency, but the unit could be activated if the country is at war.

In 1980 I was introduced into cocaine a drug that would bring me down so fast I wouldn't know what hit me. I attended my weekend drills with the National Guard, but that also meant, I was back in New York with the crew. Cocaine is a drug that keeps you up and you are never tired it gives you lots of energy and during sex it can keep you active for a long time, many women would be satisfied or tiered, some women loved cocaine. If you met up with one at a club and had some—cocaine, you had a very good chance of going home or to a hotel with her. Who needed a girl friend? You can get a different one every week, and that's exactly what I did.

I would make money playing dice, and working. America was pretty much doing coke. I found a job downtown Manhattan by the world trade center working as a foot messenger. I would take mail to offices, banks, wherever it needed to go same day mail. Right outside the World Trade Center there was a park and there was a black guy selling drugs. One day as I was passing by I saw a white man wearing a suit the type you think was decent and respectable, buying drugs from the dealer. I said no way he's a Professional! Well dressed white man, why is he's buying drugs from that black kid? You see where I grew up, it was blacks and Puerto Ricans and some poor whites, your typical well dressed with a suit white man was the one you would mug. So you could buy drugs and get high. Wow was I stupid! as I may sound I was really confused. Working in Manhattan, I learned and saw a lot of wrong things going on. I started to learn about how everybody is riding the same boat, some just know how to hide and be a hypocrite, along with pretending to be God's gift to the world.

One night we went to a party and a couple of our crew members went to buy some cocaine one of them was shot, because of an argument while buying the cocaine. We went to the hospital to visit him and he was ok, but his arm was broke from the Bullitt and the shell was still in his arm. I was furious and wanted payback in a big way. A couple of days later an old friend of mine, a matter of fact" It was my Vice Pres. from the Baby Spades. He was driving a truck, so I told him what happen to Robert, and we packed the truck with people and went up to Watson to beat up the guy who shot our crew member. I got out of the truck and grabbed the first guy who was on the corner selling drugs and punched him so hard he dropped down to the ground his eyes were fearful for he saw a raging bull come at him, then I stomped him along with another friend. I was crazy. Crazy because this was a cocaine drug spot which meant it was someone's business, and the owner was known to be a real rough neck. I was grabbed by one of the boys and was told lets go. So I kicked the guy one more time and I said you ever touch my brother again, it will be worse next time. We went back to the projects and drank some beer and snorted some coke, a car full of drug dealers came to the projects looking for me and mousy. I went right after them no gun nothing, just my heart and fist, that's all I had. I never owned a gun; I was old school fight with your hands and live to fight another day. I had allot of hate, but never wanted to kill anyone, all along I was fighting my own people how enslaved I was.

They told us they come in peace and wanted to clear the problem so we got in the car with them and as soon as I went into the building The head man in charge pulled out a gun on me and said 'I'm going to blow your Fucking head off" I knew there was nowhere to run, so I looked right at him and stood quit, Jake jumped in front and said no". Jake was mousy older brother and he had much pull, he would broker the meeting. I was giving a pass, eye for an eye, we did not go to rob them, just get revenge for our brother, "The law of the Ghetto" I now looked at death for the second time and said to myself that eventually God will be busy and won't be able to help me one day.

The club we partied at was called the last call, a club that would open at 4 am and close at 12 Afternoon. I was starting to develop a habit of being in the streets for 2-3 days without going home just going after the drugs. I would go change somewhere and continue. I was starting to become a bum and I was only 19, any money I got was for cocaine. I did not care about myself anymore just the drug. The good thing was after it wore off you could go to sleep. Cocaine was only addictive when you used it—it wasn't like heroin. Heroin was a drug I did not want to use, many of my friends became heroin addicts and some died of aids, and some wear strung out big time. Cocaine gave you time to think once it wore off. One day my brother Jose told me about this job with the city of NY. I was lucky I didn't have any felonies or Jail time other than those 1 nighters I spent in a cell. I went to 49 Thomas Street in Manhattan and put in my application it was a civil service job with union benefits. I took a test and I passed it. The job was a custodian job which meant cleaning toilets, hallways, offices, I didn't care, I took the job. I told my friends, but they did not want to work. My friend tony got himself a good job with city housing. A plasterer helper that paid very good and also had a great union with benefits.

One time I needed a tooth pulled my back tooth, I did not have medical insurance at the time so I went to the hospital and they took care of me. A few weeks later I got a letter from Social Services offering me welfare benefits, I told them to keep it shove up there rear. This is one Puerto Rican who did not take one penny from welfare. They actually told me I had to take it. I said no! I don't want it. I said if you want to? Give it to a loser I just didn't like the effect welfare had on people although I was a low down junkie, I felt that the system was wrong, there is no reason for any man to accept welfare, but there are circumstances when one does need it! I had no kids no problems; all I needed was a pulled tooth. The government has exploited people with welfare for many years. Subsequently, there are people that are currently depending on public assistance. The question is: who has the fault in this matter?

The ghetto was full of free money why? So that people could get on their feet, or keep them down, and lazy. Medicaid is the only assistance I believe in, all people should have health care in this country, Men on food stamps is ridiculous. I never believed in that type of help, when you give people money without any effort on their behalf, it makes them lazy and clueless about what a man suppose to be. I'm not trying to be cruel, but people need to learn that free has another meaning. When Jesus was with his apostles fishing and they couldn't catch any fish he said throw the nets on the other side and there was the fish. People have to earn it, however this country also has to provide jobs for all people so food doesn't become a problem. We are all at fault. I'm not saying if someone is struggling you don't help them, I'm talking about the self seeker who is lazy and has no goals, just sleep, eat, and collect welfare.

Woman also take advantage of the welfare system; getting pregnant than throwing the responsibility on the tax payer. I hold the men accountable for that, but when the government is offering free money what do you expect people to do. If you are walking and found a suitcase with a million dollars and no address what would the average person do? Hand it over to the police, sure" that is exactly the way people look at welfare. So why does the government give away something, then their pissed that it's being taken advantage off? The answer is? They want to keep people from growing. They want to control you, and they sit in front of their TV set saying look how we take care of these people, but what they are doing is exploiting them.

The eighties were wild it would be my last decade as a lost soul. I would die and be reborn by 1991, however there will be more years left of misery so let me tell you what happen 80-82 it was total chaos cocaine was really the drug of choice for many and aids was already an epidemic, although Ronald Reagan did not do a thing about it till 1986. People thought that aids was just for gays and heroin users. But that was false people who needed transfusions, were getting infected with the disease. The blood bank did not screen the blood they were getting from donors. Who were the donors, mostly, heroin addicts, drug users people selling blood for money. Money was moving in the right direction for the rich Wall Street was booming and America was drinking Champagne and snorting cocaine, and like the housing market crash of the 2000s we were creating a drug epidemic and aids disease that would cost us millions in healthcare. When money is moving the world becomes blind to the little things that are really big things in transition. Ronald Reagan did do a good job with the military, which was the most underpaid job in America. If only he would of come a little more to the left he would have gotten 100. Their were problems in El Salvador, Nicaragua, and like always here comes the US to make things better as the *Santanistas* tried to overthrow *Somoza*, who was the leader of Nicaragua and a real dictator. We helped Somoza with arms and intelligence.

I would go to my National Guard drills and every summer we would spend 2weeks in Fort Drum New York, so we could play soldier. I fired the 105 howitzer cannon and it was great. I had a lot of fun driving up in a jeep all the way to Watertown NY. I remember on my dad's bus rides when I was young I was amazed looking at the National Guard Troops driving on the highway with their duce in half trucks, jeeps, water buffalo, etc. Here I am so many years later doing the same. The law of attraction is very true whenever you like something eventually you will get it. I really liked army life for the very little time I would portray it. I should have gotten my GED.

My hanging out and parading around with my crew was getting dull, the fun in getting high was different than before I was chasing not enjoying. Drugs are like a restaurant you go the first time and the food is perfect, than you find yourself chasing that first taste, it never comes, so it becomes insanity. It's amazing how the addict finds energy to continue looking for that feeling he never gets, but never gives up trying to achieve it. It just to show you how much drive we have, and did I have plenty of it. I would walk for blocks looking for someone to lend me money so I can buy drugs." Yo man" I need 20 dollars I will pay you on Friday". That was it; my life throughout my addiction. 1982 would come in and that would be a real good year for me comes September. I got a call from the City, the job I took the test for called me for an interview. I met some representatives of one of the locations in the city looking for help. It was a Community College in the Bronx named after Eugenio Maria de *Hostos,*

Hostos was born 1839 in Puerto Rico and studied in Spain he was active in Republican politics in Spain, but left in 1869 when Spain new constitution refused to give autonomy to Puerto Rico, He would leave Spain and go to the US where he became Editor of the Cuban independence *Journal La Revolución* in 1870. He traveled throughout South America and Taught in Chile. He returned to the US hoping that Puerto Rico would become independent, but as we all know today that didn't happen. He went to the Dominican Republic were he got involved in the educational system. He later died on August 11, 1903. It's a shame how many Puerto Ricans wanted Independence, what prideful person wouldn't! How would we act if China took over and we had to drop our flag and customs and follow a new order of Government, I understand Dr. Campos" why he fought for Independence, no one wants to be ruled by a foreign Government.

Hostos Community College was like being in Puerto Rico or Santo Domingo. The classes were all in Spanish because most students didn't know English. So it was like they had to teach in Spanish to teach English. I know one Spanish professor who would off loved to teach there. I was 22 years old the youngest of the custodians, I looked more like a student than a custodian. Meringue was the new dance; it wasn't that hard to learn neither. I would learn how to dance it quick, in order for me to party with the students on Friday nights. Dominican woman were coming from all sides and where very aggressive with their looks, and a lot of us Puerto Rican guys were hot for them. Puerto Rican woman also are beautiful, the problem was that most Nuyorican woman were Americanized, Dominican woman were coming with a strong Latin accent, and dressing very sexy. Dominican men were sporting Puerto Rican woman, Puerto Rican guys sporting Dominican woman. It was the best job I ever had hot looking woman all over the place along with my Latin brothers and sisters, it was paradise for a Puerto Rican. My supervisor name was Steven D. and Rod was the foreman. My job was to clean classrooms, and bathrooms, hallways, etc I had tremendous benefits, and union dues were only 12 bucks a payday. My salary was about 12,000 a year some people don't even make that today in Hampton roads. We only worked from Monday thru Friday and I had the good shift 3:30pm to midnight. That gave me all morning to sleep. I said to myself I had to change, because I did not want to lose this job. I would get a fresh start, new people new area, so I could leave that bum in Bronx River. I stopped hanging out with my homeboys and started hanging with Dominicans, and Puerto Ricans, from the school although there were more Dominicans than Puerto Rican students the staff was pretty much Puerto Rican.

The students were fun to be with most were Legal aliens, looking for a better way of life. Unfortunately cocaine didn't go away the school was on 149th street and Grand concourse. I of course would find were to buy it, but, I maintained a positive attitude and within 6 months I became the Shop Steward. The job of the shop steward is to relay all union information to the workers. You are a representative of the union, if someone is in trouble you council him or her and help them. I was a mouth! So everybody picked me when the union rep. showed up, looking for a new Shop Steward. I enjoyed that job because it gave me a lot of power, something I liked. If there was a problem, I had to be informed, if they wanted to fire somebody they had to ask me, anything that had to do with the employees I was involved. What a rep. the biggest coke head in the building. They didn't know me yet; because I was very good hiding my addiction. I was starting to control or just not do that much coke, because I was working and I knew how crazy I would get when I sorted it.

82 would end and here comes 1983, this was the year I met Malta she worked at the college as a security Guard, I believe that was sexy, but we got along fine. We started dating and love was starting to appear in my hated life. I didn't do any hits of cocaine at all when I was with her. I really liked her a lot and her parents liked me also. Another good trait of mine every girl I had I always got along good with the parents, "you see" I was old school if you bought Chinese

food you better bring dad a wing, because he was going to ask, I would talk to them and show them respect all the time. I was still pretty much a Bronx River b-boy, but Malta would go with me to buy clothes on payday. The clothes gave me more off a Puerto Rican look. You see Bronx River was dominated by Blacks so I wore and sported there style of dressing. I started combing my hair backwards instead of getting the short haircut. I was starting to look like a real Rican. Instead of wearing sneakers all the time I wore shoes and dress paints not that the brothers didn't wear shoes and dress pants, but it was different.

The new dance in RB was *darle huevo* it was pretty stupid, but it was the dance Lisa—Lisa and cult jam. Brenda Star, up in coming Puerto Rican singers in R&B music. Disco was also carrying over from the 70s Salsa was great so was meringue Wifredo Vargas, Conjunto Quesqeya, Bobby valentine, El Gran Combo, Hector Lavoe, from the 70s and so on. We go dancing on the weekends and I remember a night we got pretty drunk and laughed as we walked home, I was the kind of guy who would love to just have fun with a girl joke laugh have a real good time. I enjoyed that. I can't stand girls who walk with their asses on their shoulders. Like they are God's gift to the planet, give me a nice regular lady and I will show you how to enjoy her company. Malta was a very pretty, dark colored Puerto Rican princess, she had the body of a great dancer which she was and I was ready to marry her if it came to that. I actually saw myself going straight home after I left her, at her home. She lived in Jackson Avenue and had 2 brothers and 1 sister. I really felt good being around her. When at the job I would look for her and ask if she ate something or if she wanted something. What I could not understand was why the drug wasn't calling me? like in the past. Maybe I was in love with this girl. Cocaine wasn't addictive only when you used it, and that depends on the person tolerance for the drug. When the mind has a change in thinking it could stay away from all impulses, but the plan has to be followed up with more tools. I will explain this to you much more later. Our relationship was great and I enjoyed every moment of it.

One night we went out together with the parents. We got back late about 3 am, that is not a good time to be walking around Jackson Avenue, so I spent the night in her room. I did not touch her out of respect for her dad. I hated myself, because I really wanted her, but the time wasn't right. Some woman you could have relations with anywhere! However I wanted it to be special with her. Doing it in a room next to her dad's room was not going to be special. I guess the drug did call me one day, but it did it in another way. One day on my daily routine walk around the school looking for Malta to see what we would have for lunch. I saw her making a call on the public phone. I listen to her I was eased dropping on her conversation. I remember hearing; I will see you at 11; 30 pm. My heart and my world just dropped ALTHOUGH I DID NOT HAVE THE FACTS another guy was my first thought. That night I took her home. She quickly jumped into the shower, I was falling apart inside, but like my worse trait

I was afraid to ask. So I told her good night and went on to meet my partner's beer and some coca. I would be missing for 3 days. I was just going from place to place getting high. It was my first puppy love or whatever you call it. Since I was a dramatic person, I expected her to come running into my arms with a relieved feeling that I was ok. Unfortunately not in the hood, only in white movies, I got home and my mom was worried and my farther, but I did not see Malta. I told my dad what happen and he said "WHAT' ALL THIS OVER SOME WOMAN" what happen to the tough guy Tyrone gang member. I went to work and saw her and we talked, but she decided to leave me. So I would felt bad, but would go on with my job and met other girls. I did not give them the same attention I gave Malta. I became very nasty with my attitude and did not get close to any of them. I did not want that feeling again.

I was angry and drinking took a large part of my life. I remember one time getting paid and spending all my money in 1 night on cocaine and drinking, then having to go 2 weeks before payday again. So I started to develop bar tabs, and cocaine, on credit and also at the package store. On payday, I had people lined up ready to get paid by me; it would leave me with very little money left so by 10 pm that night I was broke again. I was getting worse and I was only 22 years old. I was acting and becoming a bum with a Job. I was able to keep my lifestyle quiet because a lot of employees also got high on coke, but I was starting to ask other workers for a loan since I was new and just getting over a relationship { how full of shit I was] people would lend me the money. It was the summer but 83 would have more obstacles and I would continue to sink as low as anyone can. I was no longer getting embarrassed. I just wanted the drug. I would show signs of change and hope would fill my spirit, but my rollercoaster ride wasn't over. I would have a mountain to climb that looked never ending. Well after I found out that my girl Malta was just going to do her friends hair, I felt very dumb.

Chapter 3

New York. Everybody loved it, it was called, the city that never sleeps; with all the cocaine we snorted how could we. There was always something to do in NY, we had all the major sports in NYC, The Jets, Giants, Mets, Yankees, Knicks, Nets, the hockey team of the 80s Islanders, Rangers, and devils. We also had Broadway, the theater, great hotels, and all the luxury you wanted. You would not have to leave the city in order to have fun. I am a Met, and Jets, fan I joined that fan club in 1969 when I was 8years old why? Joe Namath, QB for the Jets and Tom Seaver, Pitcher for the Mets, where the anchors of both teams, In 1969 they beat a powerful Baltimore Colts team and Baltimore Orioles, In the Super Bowl and World Series. Of course Roberto Clemente was the man for us Puerto Ricans, or any real baseball fan, you had to admire him. He died in a plane crash taking supplies over to Nicaragua. He would be remembered for his generosity and Great play. Going back to the 70s I remember asking my Dad to buy me a Joe Namath football Uniform, they cost about 10 bucks at John bargains store in the Bronx or Woolworths, me and my friend Anthony would get the uniforms, We were very happy with our new toy. We put it on and went to play this team from building 1595 they had KC chiefs Uniforms and beat the living daylights out of us. However we would still support our Jet uniforms, because win or lose you never turn your back on the team. Of course I'm still waiting for the Jets to win another Super Bowl, let see what Rex Ryan does ironically his dad was a coach on the Jets Super bowl team, Buddy Ryan.

I was also part of the Sea Cadets when I was between the ages of 9, 10, 11. We were drilled by ex military veterans that were training us, we wore The Navy dressed uniform and drilled, and we also had a band. I played the bass drum, tenor, and snare. I was very good at it also. How military life followed me. I was in several parades. I remember my dad laughing when he saw me with a drum bigger than me, the Bass drum as I was marching and hitting it Boom, boom. He was really proud, before I left Grammar school I won a trophy for being on the All Star Basketball team. When I look back at my young life my parents set me up for success and I failed them, I mean I was a Cadet, played Basketball, football, baseball, was very fast in track & field. I pass my co-op, test which allowed me admittance in a great catholic High School. I gave all that up for 1 bad day in the first grade. How can I allow myself to be so weak minded. That Nun/ teacher brought out the worse in me. Holding own to resentments can cause cancer of the soul, we do it every day! we inherit grudges and then want to lie around in self pity boo hoo hoo!!. Why as people do we torture ourselves so much? There were other students that got smacked around also back in those days; schools were notorious for beating students. Tyrone? Yes! What's the answer for no 1? 3, no! "Smack" hate would be our education, and I was in the middle of it all, all of us were. I lived with Blacks, Puerto Ricans, and went to school with whites or Italians, Irish, German, Polish, Greek. There was 1 black girl called Gail that was it in my class, there was another, but I don't remember, but do remember how I was out numbered and had to learn how to adapt.

Throughout the 60s, 70s, all you herd was racial remarks, and here's the kicker! At times Blacks were just as racial to Puerto Ricans and Puerto Ricans back to them, the only problem was; we had to share neighborhoods together and white America looked at us the same way. A matter of fact it was blacks and Puerto Ricans That were killing each other and calling each other niggers, by the early seventies white boys were not coming in to our neighborhoods looking for trouble. While the white man was getting rich up on Wall Street, It was us who were controlled mentally to destroy our homes and imprison our people with crime. Our ignorance is our biggest enemy, not the white Man. We failed to observe that. I was one of them! So I'm also a fool.

The Black Panthers, and Young lords, were organizations that tried to teach the community and give us knowledge of our rights as Americans, but like always our ignorance kept us enslaved. J. Edgar Hoover made sure that wouldn't happen." OH' wait a minute white man" I'm not letting you off the hook yet. I do admire you. You are very smart and know how to turn people against each other. You even Had Puerto Ricans Killing Puerto Ricans in the massacre of Ponce. But is it the white man? Or is it another group which is making this turbulence in order to keep us asleep? I'm sorry my brothers! ; But not all white people are bad, and not all Latinos, and African Americans, good! However they allow us to destroy ourselves by selling drugs to each other; you could sell drugs like a store sells candy in your neighborhood. I believe all people are the same we are just culturally diverse, but are we? When doctors study the human body there is not a study for every race just one, the human.

In September of 1983 I would meet a young Dominican lady called Marisa she was fresh from Santo Domingo and it was me who she liked. Her friend Angela gave me the news that she wanted to meet me and I went to see her in the cafeteria. She spoke no English, so I had to speak Spanish constantly to be able to have a conversation. I knew how to speak it, but not on her level. I had no idea what she saw in me, she was pure, good, and was very easy to manipulate. Why was I like that with such a nice girl? She would be my first Latina girl from the Islands, maybe my bad experience with romance with Malta turned me into a monster?

But it was the cocaine and alcohol that turned me into a monster, sorry Malta I can't give you anymore props.

She invited me to her home and I went, Of course! With my mind full of lust and ready to have some fun, however, it wasn't about that, she wanted to cook me something traditional. How low can I be! I said Ok. She bought some plantains, cheese, for frying and Salami, at the local market. There was a nice deli next door and I asked her if she preferred to have a roast beef sandwich? She said "no" I don't want that, I want to make you lunch. I'm thinking hum" salami, Plantains, Cheese, what is she going to make?, well it turned out to be dish called *Mangu* It was ok the cheese, and Salami, was great, but I did not like the plantains. The plantains boiled than smashed into and formed in a round shape. Our afternoon was good and I felt positive I had something sweet and special with Marisa. Unfortunately my drug and alcohol problem was getting worse and I was losing control.

The Dominicans took over the city quick Drugs and businesses. Most Puerto Ricans were moving out and selling their bodegas, properties, business, and moving back to Puerto Rico, or Florida. A new regime took over and they took no prisoners. Not all Dominicans were following the fast pace of NY life; they like many other immigrants who arrive in America looking for a better life had 2 choices crime or honesty. Marisa's Mom Juliana was a hard working woman who would work 3 Jobs if you gave it to her. Immigrants are always split in half good and bad, everybody comes here to find a better way of life. The world knows it, going back to the first European, who evaded their own country in order to form Governments here in America. You think Native Indians were ripped off, because these people were just bad! No! Because opportunity was here for them to grow and have the chances they couldn't have in their own countries. The blood spilled over it was devastating! The Civil War Whites killing whites using slavery as an excuse when all along it was the country they were fighting over. The Irish was another Race that got smacked around, as soon as they got off the boat at Ellis Island in NY harbor, they were told to go fight for the country. These people didn't even know what they were fighting over, but they did the job, and then got exploited by the Americans who forgot that at one time were immigrants themselves.

Marisa had 2 sisters Areles and Miosotis. I got along with both of them fine although it would be Arelis who will teach me how to dance meringue, Boy! I danced meringue very well. I would learn salsa later. In the 80s it was all about meringue in NY. Salsa was not doing so well, meringue was an easy dance to learn, meringue was the big thing back then. They would play salsa and very little would dance, then here comes a meringue and everybody is dancing. They would have parties almost every Sunday at Marisa's house, Arelis would cook something very good and have some beer to drink or My best Dominican drink *Macoris,* or *Barcelo anejo* and the beer was *Presidente.* I was starting to get back into my Latin roots a little more, a lot of Spanish speaking and Caribbean food would fill my life with happiness and excitement. I tell you there is no better culture than the Latin culture, Puerto Rican, Dominican, Cuban, Mexican, etc is all good. I would love one day for all Latin people to share and experience unity and have one big feast. Everybody loves our food, and drinks, and maybe it's because Latin people are part of all races, African, European, Indian, maybe even Asian. We bring much diversity to the table, and it's hard to ignore our culture.

When Marisa and I were at the school we did not talk much. I was working and I was plotting on getting high on cocaine most of the time. There was a lot of drinking going on with the custodians so it wasn't hard for me to hide my addiction. I was getting to the point where all I did was a little bit of my job and I was done. My work area was starting to look bad and my boss had to bring it up to my attention several times, but he was fair and understood that I was young and maybe I would come around and do better. Marisa and I would start seeing a lot more of each other and I would continue with my addiction. On day there was a Christmas party at the school for the staff. That week a nice girl from Puerto Rico had arrived to NY and my God parents asked me to take her out, I did not want to say no so I invited her to the staff party, since Marisa was a student, I couldn't invite her because I was not suppose to get have personal relations with any students. It was a good excuse. I can't remember her name, but she graduated from college in Puerto Rico and was coming to NY to start work. Something Puerto Ricans need to stop doing! "We need to build Puerto Rico"

So I bring her through the back entrance of the college and take her to the party. We sit down at a table and we talk. A few minutes later the security guard who was working the door came to my table and asks, if he could have a word with me? I excused myself, and ask what he wanted? He said that Marisa was asking if she could come in to the party. She knows you are in here. I would have to escort her if I wanted her to participate. I quickly said "no"! I got nervous. I went outside and told her that she could get me in trouble. That it was a staff party I can't bring you inside because I'm not to have personal relations with any student. She went away sad and I would go back to my date. We continue talking and a few minutes later here comes the security guard again saying that Marisa wants to come inside, you really need to go talk to her. You see everybody knew that we were going out with each other, it was just me. I was being the real jerk. I went out to talk to her and she started telling me that she has seen students go into the party with staff members and I wasn't being honest with her. So I told her that I didn't want to take the chance. I go back in and the other girl is starting to notice something strange about the way I was acting, I mean you did not have to be a rocket scientist to figure out what was going on. I told her that I was in charge tonight and that any problems I would be called. She believed me, but here comes the Security guard again for the third time. I said what the hell! I give up. I told her I was with another woman inside, but it was just a favor I was doing for my Godmother. She started to cry and when I tried to show affection she threw a punch at me out of anger or maybe disappointment that I had failed to be the guy she wanted me to be. She left and went back to Santo Domingo the next day for the holidays. I went back into the party, then my date was pissed and she told me she was leaving so that left me alone with no girlfriend, no date, just my best friend, alcohol, and cocaine, which I did and went on a 3 day bender. I would listen to the song "It takes a fool "by the spinners. 1983 would finish with me just getting high and destroying myself even more I felt very bad and accepted my punishment. I drank it down with lots and lots of Bacardi.

1983 ended up pretty bad, I would lose 2 gorgeous woman from the Island's one from Puerto Rico and one from Santo Domingo, But all was not lost in that same year I experienced` some political moments like the Black and Puerto Rican caucus, That was nothing, but pure politics. Drinking, socializing, and having fun. We stood at the Hilton Hotel in Albany NY. I would party with politicians and Union leaders. Ronald Reagan was leading in the polls nobody wanted change, because to be honest the stock market was up and doing well Reagan brought fear to the Middle East as soon as he became President. Iran who in 1979 under The Jimmy Carter administration stormed and took over the American Embassy in Tehran than when Reagan won the Presidency the Iranians let the hostages go. Our military forces were getting stronger and the Star Wars program would be the hot topic. The idea was to battle the Russians economically and bankrupt them. I believe it was a better idea than having a nuclear war. Unfortunately many programs in NY were cut due to Reagan's plan. As a person that was living in the ghetto at that time, I can assure you that some of these programs were a waste of money. Drugs, gangs, and hate were the dilemma, social programs were not the answer and as I go on you will understand why I feel this way.

In order for a country to be strong it needs strong military, jobs for the people in order for them to spend so everyone could capitalize. The US is a country that the least amount of money someone should be making is 60.000 a year. The opportunity was there yes; there is always racism and people keeping you down, however I remember when black's did not give respect to the Puerto Rican Needs, they hogged up all the summer Jobs and housing projects apartments, throughout the city and treated us like crap, It's to show you what happens when things change. The oppress could become just like the oppressor. I'm not trying to go against my African American brother, but I am not here to lie neither. We all have faults in life and we are not perfect and capitalism was invented to turn the people on each other while others prosper from their ignorance. Puerto Ricans also struggled, with the want to be white attitude. I mean anything with blue eyes and blond hair was God. I got so sick of hearing that one day I told my mother why do you admire those people who keep us downs o much? She said, we are white not Black, I said, well! White people must be color blind because I surely don't get the respect I deserve from them like they respect each other. The problem is, Puerto Ricans are white, Black, Brown, and they are because of the diversity within Latin America. They really could be just as segregated in Puerto Rico then in the US. Latin people are the most racial people in the world, I hate to say it, but there are. I remember My mom saying "*no te casar con una negra porque dañar la raza*" It meant don't marry into the black race, because it would destroy our race. That is Spain talking, not Puerto Ricans, however Blacks felt like this at one time also. I remember the Movie with Sidney Poitier" look who's coming for dinner" the black maid was more upset that the Black man who was a doctor! was not good enough for the white woman he loved, she right away felt he had something up his sleeve, I'm not trying to justify here but, do I get my point across, we are all victims of some kind of mental slavery from our upbringing. Therefore we all suffer from the same problem rejection.

1984 would be a big year for me and it was also be another term for the President. Walter Mondale and Geraldine Ferraro would be the democratic candidates, and lose. Ronald Reagan and George Bush would return for a second term. Aids was growing and becoming a social problem and Crack cocaine was on the streets. Violence and drive by shootings were taking place in America. Right outside the White House you could see the drug deals going on. Mostly in black and Latino neighborhoods, Crack dealers were taking over buildings children dying from gunshot wounds the city was a real mess, even the Mayor of Washington DC was accused of smoking crack. This was a real problem, but Reagan did not care, he was so focused on the star wars program and making America the big boys on the block. In his campaign he said that "the only increase I will approve is in our military" that sound good into the ears of Casper Weinberger who was Secretary Of Defense under Reagan. That blew doom into the Democratic Party's ears. America was getting stronger in one faze but weaker in another. The Movie New Jack city was in the eyes of ghetto people: for they saw themselves battling a war in their own streets. They were finding the great American dream in selling crack true Ghetto capitalism at is best! That drug was so strong that you could turn someone out with one puff; they would be back for more even if it meant stealing from loved ones. I would be introduced into it, but did not like it at first. Crack Cocaine was cooked into pure cocaine then put in a glass pipe, then with a lighter placed against the cocaine rock it would burn and you smoke it, the feeling was devastating and forced you into wanting more. It was really called freebasing. The first time I tried it, it made me sick and I puked! So I just kept snorting cocaine.

Marisa came back from Santo Domingo in January of 1984 to start the semester and her friend came to me and said she wanted to see me in the cafeteria. I guess she did not take heed to the first round of Tyrone! What was she thinking? Or was this just pure destiny? We talked and I apologized for being the jerk I was. I was always apologizing only because I knew my life was wrong; however I didn't have the power to change. I was so addicted to drinking and drugging that when I try to stop my change wouldn't last long. Occasionally I would take a hit of Cocaine and stop; I felt if I just drank alcohol all would be fine. That is what I did. Every weekend we were together having fun and being with family. My Spanish would get better and I couldn't shut up, because I am a talker. I would offend people, because I did not know what I was saying half the time it just sounded good so I went with it. I was not putting the words in the right format for smart conversation. One day while waiting for the train Marisa tells me she's pregnant. I didn't know what to think, but happiness was the feeling. I said, let's get married. My family was happy that I was getting married and that a baby was on its way. They did worry that for how long would Marisa hold on, or would I change, because I was going to be a father.

We started to plan the wedding which would take place on July 28th 1984 the hall we rented was right down the block from the College where I worked and she studied. The place was called the Savoy Manor. I was very happy, because I always dreamed of having a family of my own so I started praying to God and asking him to please help me to get sober or to control my habits. I got a loan for $ 3.500.00, but spent 500 getting high and gave my wife or future wife the rest. She ask me what happen to the other 500 dollars, I said they only gave me 3000.00. She believed me and we went rented the hall and put a down payment on the catering, plus 3 limos, for the wedding party. Primo a friend of Marisa's mother brought all the alcohol. We also got a DJ this was a big wedding all together we spent 10.000 dollars. The wedding was a big hit a lot of people came and we partied till 4 am. I was so drunk I didn't want to leave the party. One thing we failed to do is put money away for a honeymoon; we were flat broke, but did get some money gifts, at the wedding, plus a lot of toasters and blenders. One of the guests offered to take me and my wife to a hotel in Jersey for the night. We went and he left us and said he would pick us up at 11 am he did not come to get us, I didn't neither, I was so drunk that when I got to the hotel I fell asleep with my tuxedo on. That was really a bad start to a marriage.

We get up in the morning and I tell her, were we going to live? I mean we just planned the wedding and not once I thought about getting an apartment. We looked at each other like boy are we dumb!! So she says well I'll go home and you do the same until we find an apartment. I said no! You are my wife, and you are carrying my child we will stay with my parents till we could move into our own place. I was not your typical jerk off guy who wants to have sex with a woman then let someone else take care of my responsibility's, drunk or no drunk I will take care of my child and my wife. My heart was in the right place, but my head wasn't my drug abuse would continue. We found a place in 207 Street in Manhattan Dykman Ave. Not so far from Washington Heights, little Santo Domingo. We stayed there for 4 months, and a friend helped get me an apartment in the Bronx 2160 Walton Avenue, the apartment was rented before, by a drug dealer so people would knock on the door looking to buy drugs. I thought of making an investment, but felt I would just use it all and not make any money.

When I used drugs; I would leave for days 2-3 days and my wife would suffer wondering where I was. I would always make up some crazy lie. Before 84 would end my wife was threatening to leave me. I would tell her that I would change, this is just a bad time for me please don't leave me. 85 came in and I was very excited to find out what I was getting? A boy or girl, Of course I wanted a boy, but whatever it was I was ok with it. Well the big day came and I was very cool about it, my wife water broke so very carefully I took her to the car and brought her to the hospital it was Tuesday March 5, 1985 7pm. I went into the room with her and watched her scream and yell while the baby was born. It was a girl, I named her Jeanette. She would save my life many times. My Daughter is the reason I am alive today, however it would be awhile before that happen.

I was crazy about Jeanette I play with her, look at her, I was just happy. On the 4th day of her life I decided to take my family back to Bronx River my parent's apartment. Even though I was crazy about my new born baby I was still drinking and using cocaine. Living in my parents' house would assure me that my wife and daughter would be safer than in the apartment we had on Walton Avenue. On certain occasions I would leave the house at 2 am to go get high. It would start off with a drink then I would start getting thoughts of how good a hit of coca would be. I go get it then instead of going back home I would snort it all up and then wanted some more. I was also getting into crack; I tried it again and was starting to like it. So the move back to my mother house was smart. I was always thinking of the safety of my wife and kid. I remember one time in a prayer I asked God; why can't I live my life normal like other people? Off course I wouldn't get an answer. I always believed that I will find a hole and sneak right through it and find peace and happiness. This wild life of mine was temporary.

I would get sober or fight to stay sober, Whenever Jeanette needed to go to the doctor. I provided medical coverage for my daughter and my wife. My mother would take care of Jeanette while I worked and Marisa was going to school. In early June I really pissed her off, I went on a 3 day bender and she was getting ready to leave with Jeanette, I cried and said please don't leave and she said I have giving you too many chances and you don't change. Again I talked her into staying. I knew how much she like going to Santo Domingo so I bought us a couple of tickets to go Santo Doming for Christmas to spend 3 weeks, she was happy and would look at the tickets with a very big smile, that would buy me time. I needed to get my act together. Crack cocaine was getting out of hand and NYPD had their hands full. People were living like prisoners in their own homes, crack head people where dangerous. I remember a building I would go to that had crack apartments and people sitting around waiting for someone to give them some crack or thinking that the little white dots on the floor were pieces of crack that maybe somebody dropped. Crack was a nuclear bomb which caught the whole country by surprise, yes!! Life was getting bad in NY.

Chapter 4

The birth of my daughter gave me hope that all would be fine. I remember when I was young I thought of having a family, a car, nice place to live, like the house I saw in a neighborhood in upstate NY, Vacations to Disney, the rental car, staying in a hotel, And Puerto Rico regularly. I wanted the good life not that my family didn't provide me one, but the one you see on television, the American dream. The dream I was experiencing was the American nightmare.

One good thing was happening the New York Mets were playing great baseball along with the New York Jets playing some good football. The 1985 baseball season would end with the Mets and Cardinals in a weekend due or die for the division series at Busch Stadium. I remember the Homerun Darryl strawberry hit to win the game it silenced the crowd as he hit that ball a ton. Like always the Mets would lose in the 3rd game and would be 2 games out of first place. The acquisition of Gary Carter was the spark the Mets needed. 1986 would be another great year for Mets, Jets, fans, but the Giants would steal the show in football. The jets went 10-1 only to lose their last 5 games thanks to a certain man who jinxed us and said the Jets wouldn't win again. They got into the playoffs and beat K.C. but a brutal penalty called on Mark .G, against him in the divisional playoffs, would give the browns another chance to win. The Browns would come back to tie and win the game in double overtime. Same old jets always on the right track and blowing it at the end. Not the Mets they were cocky and did not know how to lose even when they should off. They won 108 games, and the playoffs couldn't have been any more dramatic then the Mets against the Astros and in the World Series Mets and Red Sox. My favorite call, game 6, of the 1986 RED SOX, METS World Series bottom of the tenth Vin Scully with the call, A LITTLE ROLLER UP FIRST, BEHIND THE BAG IT GET THROUGH BUCKNER HE COME KNIGHT AND THE METS WIN IT YEHHHHHHHHHHHHHH. I was going crazy in my room and was so happy I started to cry, but it was a cry of victory.

It is a great feeling when your team wins, sports is the greatest motivator in the world. The Jets in the regular season would do something similar Miami's Dan Marino and The Jets Kenny Obrien threw for over 900 yards. Here is the call from the Meadowlands in sudden death OT. Obrien back to throw he throws deep to Wesley Walker TOUCHDOWN, TOUCHDOWN, `TOUCHDOWN the Jets are going berserk they are mobbing Wesley Walker in The end zone.

That was the best moments in sports that year for Mets and Jets fans. The Giants along with, Carson, Taylor and Simms and company won the Super Bowl. It was almost a perfect year. The Knicks were also in the hunt and of course the acquisition of Patrick Ewing who was our No 1 pick in 85 from the Georgetown Hoyas, got us into the playoffs every year. The Knicks and Celtics would be the real championship.

The 80s were great but cocaine had a big impact on players, Football, Basketball, and Baseball players, would get busted for getting high on cocaine, some died before even having a shot to play in the pros. Some would get sober and some would lose it all, cocaine was not racial we were all in together. Finally Washington noticed that Aids and drugs was destroying the country and creating panic. Some interesting people were getting caught with drugs and getting infected with the aids virus. The children of upper middle class and rich people were coming into Harlem and the Bronx to buy drugs; you know white kids from Jersey or Long Island and upstate NY. It wasn't the ghetto whites, Blacks, or Puerto Rican, it was upper class white kids. Drugs love everybody it's is not racial.

Maybe drugs can teach us something? We are all the same no matter what race we are, drugs gave everyone of us the same results. Sometimes the answer to our problem is right in front of us, but we are too ignorant to see it. Ignorance towards other people's culture is our dilemma! If we could learn to coexist in America; we could be more powerful than we already are. Imagine everybody just respecting and learning from each other, financially growing, having compassion for one another instead of just for you. Businesses would grow, because people would have funds to shop and enjoy a good life. Happiness would be our way of life. When helping another country; it would be more help than self seeking. Why must we destroy ourselves with false pride and selfishness, the day may actually come when God comes down and say "you have destroyed all the resources I have giving you to be successful". "You have segregated yourselves into an evil empire of false hope to the people". It's time to build a new world. "No Christians" You are also part of the problem. We all are.

If a man believes in God and is living a good life, but not following other peoples Gods; why do we fill him with fear or guilt? Religious people can act like car salesman when preaching the word of God. "Oh you are going to hell if you don't do what I do" When Jesus was teaching he never preached the way some of these phony Jesus freaks preach. I believe God wants people to believe and have respect for each other, no matter what it is as long as they are part of happiness for all, atheist included. Not your own little inquisition trying to recruit people by passing fear, but by passing love.

What I have learned so far is that when I did drink and drug; I was able to escape from the truth of my real life and everything would be fine. I remember when I Took my first drink of alcohol, I wanted more my dad would wonder who was drinking the liquor so fast. He always blamed my older brothers who were also drinking. I felt good and did not care about the world or the problems I was inheriting. I was an alcoholic before I was even an adult.

The year of 1985 would continue the same. However we had a trip to Santo Domingo. The vacation was going to save our marriage. My wife just let it be. We would have several more arguments before December would come, but like always I would talk her into staying. December arrived and the excitement of going to my first Latin country was growing. I said to myself I have to be careful, because there was going to be a lot of temptation. I was a big womanizer. Although Marisa was of white skin she had that lovely Latin look from top to bottom. I loved Latin woman especially the dark and black haired ones the natural looking ones. The alcohol was another, and hopefully I would not find any cocaine. The day came and on we went to JFK airport to fly to our well needed vacation. The airport was a madhouse I bought the tickets from Eastern Airlines, however my wife went and exchanged them for Dominican Aviation airlines and saved 185 dollars doing so. I was aware that she exchanged the tickets. I only asked her if the planes were as good as the American Planes?, very angry she told me, yes! We even have an airport she answered sarcastically. I quickly understood that I was being a jerk and stop asking.

I was hoping they weren't serving mangu for breakfast on the plane as it was an early flight. There were people sitting on floor complaining that they have been waiting for days to get out. I very quickly got angry at my wife because several minutes later our Eastern flight was boarding, so like a good drunk I went found me a bar and got a drink, and started conversation with others that were angry over the constant delays. My wife came running to get me and said that a jumbo 450 passenger plane was on its way that we had to get closer to the gate. I said ok lets go.

One hour later they opened the doors for us to come in and like a stampede of buffalos we forced ourselves in. I had my daughter under in one arm and on my other side and a shopping bag full of gifts. It was a madhouse and Little Jeannie smiling away as I was pushing with her by my side. I must say it was not such a great experience. People shouting, screaming, saying gets the bleep out of my way. We would get on the plane and everyone was happy the lady sitting next to us who had the dirtiest mouth turned out to be very nice. I guess 2days at JFK will turn anyone insane. The flight was beautiful as we cross over to the Caribbean; it reminded me of when I was a baby going to Puerto Rico. looking out the window as the Caribbean sun shined on my face. I wasn't home yet, but I felt peace. I would be around the same people. As we walked to get our luggage, I saw a different world. Everybody was speaking Spanish and a little *Paranda* (musicians) to welcome us; along with a shot of rum. I really loved that and I felt welcomed. I said these are my people. We were picked up by a family member then taking to a nice house. I was staying in *el 27 de Febrero la capital*. That night a family member took me to meet a lady and I was confused about that, since I was married to his sister in law. I wasn't in Santo Domingo 4 hours. I had planted my seed. Boy what a way to start a vacation, that was suppose to fix our marriage. He took me to his home where we were staying. I guess it was tradition since Latin men could be Male Chauvinist. Well I didn't want to offend anyone so I guess thank you, not a bad tradition at the time, I would disapprove of that today.

The house was very nice and he had 2 girls working at the house cleaning and cooking like maids, his family was in business so they lived well. He was half Italian and half Dominican. We got along great. The funny part was when I went to the rest room there were 2 toilets; I thought one was to urinate in and the other to crap in. I shared with my wife how nice it was to have two toilets; we could use the bathroom together. She called me a name and said that was for woman to clean themselves, I said Hey you are the dummy you know we have only I bathroom, I toilet, I bath, in the PROJECTS what am I suppose to think. Everyone would laugh and I would say enjoy laughing at me is common in my life, but, I had to admit it was funny as hell.

The next day we went to the *Boca Chica* a beach that was beautiful with a large wall of rocks holding back the ocean. We would have lots of romance and things were starting to look good if any. I learned how to butter up a woman when pissed, basically because I had a lot of practice saying I'm sorry, it had become part of my marriage vocabulary most married men can identify. The water was blue and very clean and lots of seafood restaurants to choose from. I was really living it up, and in a way I didn't want to go back to America. I wanted to make my life there No cocaine was needed. I didn't even think about it, but yes" I did drink from morning to evening. After coffee and breakfast, I was having a drink. I would talk a lot to the two girls that worked there, but on a respectable level. One was very religious and the other was just very kind, but Curious. I shared with them about America how they were not missing anything; that it was all overrated. This right here is paradise. I remember taking one of them out for dinner and dancing as a friend and my wife allowed me. I guess our marriage was over anyway, so she really did not care. I took her to a fancy club in Santo Domingo. We danced and had a great time and like a gentleman, I took her home untouched. We talked about it the next day and she was very excited. I felt good to see her happy, it's like hitting the lottery when you do something nice for someone without wanting something in return. I did show signs of being a real human.

Me and Marisa and Jeanette would then go to the country to visit more family *el cibao*. It was like a little town in the mountains, as I try to remember. It looked like a Tiano village they had the kitchen, separate from the sleeping area, and the living room, had like bamboo branches for a roof we ate *Sancocho*. I really liked it up there, because everything was natural, but life was hard. However they don't get lots of bills in the mailbox like we do. Their society works for survival not materialism. We would go back that night and guess who shows up? My good friend Ramon who was dating my sister-in-law Arelis, Arelis was also vacationing in Santo Domingo. He came with several friends from Puerto Rico and asked me if I wanted to hang out with them? I did and was gone for 3 days. We were partying in the *Milicon. The milicon,* a strip by the beach where you dance, eat, and have lots of fun. I enjoyed Santo Domingo. I would party everyday till we left in January. How I didn't destroy my liver I have no idea.

I loved to eat the *Chimi churris* which is a hamburger, in one night I ate 5 of them. With all that; it looked like my wife had giving up. She gave me the freedom to do what I wanted. She questioned were I was, but knew I was a lost case; she could accept it or just let me go. My love for alcohol was stronger than my love for the family. The weird thing is, when I did not drink I was the nicest person in the world caring, generous, romantic everything a man could be when at his best. But the moment I took a drink I just became different, and I always believe that my wife would think she could have a part time husband. Of course that was not going to happen. We went back home and as we cross back over to America, I said well honey did you enjoy yourself? She looked at me and actually said yes. She tells me that she has a plan, I said great.

We get home and I would tell my Mother and farther how beautiful the Dominican Republic was and that I would love to live there one day. A couple of months later my wife tried one more time to help change me, so she took me over to the Voodoo lady. I was giving a dark colored water to bathe in for 1 week. She told me that my drinking was due to a potion somebody put in my drink and they did not want to see Marisa and me together. So I said well let's do it.

I was also looking for answers to my drinking; Voodoo or Santeria was something practiced in the Latino community. Though it was more African It was born in the Caribbean. African slaves use to hide the names of their spirits in the statues of catholic saints. The week would pass and I would go to my voodoo appointment. This little lady with a cigar and something in her hand I forgot what, comes towards me and she did some type of dance and tried to wave off any evil spirits that were hurting Marisa and I and I would participate by saying, oh yes!! *espiritu sacar me esto que tengo*, ah, aha, ah, / "oh spirits take away this omen I have" it was very intense in that apartment just like in a horror movie. I really took it seriously, because I wanted to save my marriage. I did not want to lose Jeanette. I wanted to always be the only farther in her life. The session was over and we left. My wife asks me how I felt. I tried to be positive and say I feel great. That night I went on a 3 day binge. I guess my alcohol was stronger than the voodoo. My wife would leave me for the last time on April 1986 about 1 year and 8 months from marriage, Jeanette was 1 year 1 month old I was devastated. I would park my car outside were Marisa and Jeanette were staying and sleep all night there. They wouldn't know, but I would do that from time to time. Eventually within several weeks I talked Marisa into allowing my Mother and me to take care of Jeanette while she continues with her education. She agreed and I got Jeanette back, for some reason Jeanette had to be with me and not her mother.

I was single again, but now I had Jeanette. I knew eventually if I was going to be a good daddy I would have to change. In September, 1986 my daughter would have a seizure from high fever. I was called at work and told that something had happen to Jeanette; and that she was in the hospital with my mother. I rushed to the hospital with fear leading the way thinking of the worse. When I arrived at the emergency room I saw my little girl with machines around and connected to her. I wanted to drop, but I needed to find out what was happening. She would catch another convulsion and the first thing that came to my mind was it's my fault. My old religious belief quickly told me that my drug use has plagued my daughter and that punishment was eminent. Marisa arrived and we both were worried. I said we need to work out our differences for Jeanette. She told me that uniting would not do a thing for her, but that I needed to change, because we both need to work on this sickness our daughter has. I slept on the hospital floor next to my daughter, so she could see some family when getting up in the morning. The poor thing had an IV in her arm and suffered a lot. I started to get depressed because I felt it was my drug use that maybe affected her. How things were getting bad really quick. One good thing about me was, I was positive about certain situations and I knew that my daughter would live. She was later diagnosed, with epilepsy. Jeanette would have to take medicine for the rest of her life. I was devastated, but relieved that she was going to live as long as she takes her medicine. I surely believed that I would get sober over this. I would change a little and go home after work, but the moment I took a drink I was off to the races again. Whenever I took a drink of alcohol, snorted cocaine, next would be 2-3 days in the streets. I was saying to myself this has to stop, I cannot go on like this; my daughter needs me, oh please God help me. I was getting worried, because now I was smoking crack cocaine which was worse. I would steal money from my family and borrow money from people or drug dealers. Every time I got paid I owed all my money to dealers and loan sharks. I probably was the only person in the world that hated payday. Since my wife was a student still at Hostos she knew all about me and would look at me with disgust and I deserved it. I had hit a bottomless pit of shame for myself and family. I wanted to change, but alcohol had taken total control over me. I was worthless and I wanted to die so my family and ex wife would not have to see me like that anymore. My mother and farther continued to raise my daughter and Marisa would pick her up for the weekends during the semester.

In Christmas of 1986 the payday before, I said to myself I would get my little Jeannie a Christmas tree and some toys, again I would owe all my money, but decided not pay someone and with 20 dollars left fighting the inner feeling to buy drugs, I bought her a 10 dollar

Christmas Tree and a doll with a dress. I went home crying, because I felt as I hit the lowest part of my life, If it wasn't for Jeanette, I would of killed myself. I knew she would need me so I try to fight and fight, but would always get knocked down. When I got home I fix the tree with some ornaments my mom had bought and I sang Christmas carols to my lovely daughter. She was 21 months old December 1986. I would end that year miserable and tired of life. 1987 was the beginning of good things to come, on one of my 3 day benders my brother Angelo found me sitting on a street floor on Jerome Avenue and ask me, why are you doing this to yourself?. I said that I was worthless and don't deserve to live anymore. I cried on how I didn't want to live. Why is my life like this? My brother Angelo was working also at the school I had gotten him a job there when he came out of Jail he was doing good and had retain a good new beginning in society. Angelo was a heroin addict and beat his addiction while he was locked up in prison. He understood what I was going through so he helped me. He told me that I should go to rehabilitation for alcohol and drugs and see what happens.

I went to Personal at my Job and told Ronnie the personal director that I had a problem and needed help. I accepted to go to rehab. My brother Angelo would take me and when we got there the hospital said mental institution. I quickly told my brother "hey "I'm not crazy I just have a drug addiction" he looked at me, and said really!! Get your butt in there he shouts! I walked in and they closed the door. I saw people with many problems. I would be on the 4th floor with drug and alcohol abuse. Look where I wound up. 'My God why me" I talked to several doctors and counselors and was giving the message. I suffered from a disease that I had no control over, that I needed to change. A mental change or physic change as written in the "Big Book of alcoholics Anonymous". I could not believe it, there were doctors, lawyers, all kind of professional, in there for the same problem I had. The hospital was called Gracie SQ. in Manhattan 76 street. I would spend 7 days there. While in there I was told to write about my life, I did just like when I was in School. I would draw pictures and write about what happen to me in school and how the social settings affected me also.

I had time to sit and think about what was going on in my life. We had sessions where we talk and share on our experience then we would pray a little. In one of the drawings I drew a picture of myself surrounded by ugly demons, I told the counselor that it was my biggest problems. Those demons were my character defects that kept me in that state of mind and life. I was taken in a lot of knowledge of my disease which was addiction. One day they said the family could come over. I thought of calling Marisa so she and Jeanette could come over, but decided to just let it go, plus I only had 3 more days to go anyway. Some families did come over for the other patients, so I would just sit and watch them, reassuring myself that the day would come that I would have a family and would be free of this horrible life I was living.

I left the hospital and went home. I grabbed my little girl and told her things will get better for us. I would go to the outpatient program once a week and maybe 1 or 2 Narcotics Anonymous meetings. I did not work the program. All I did was read the material and I started writing my first of many journals. I started hanging out with an old time friend from when I was 7-12 years old Anthony. I was doing pretty good and was 30 days without a drink or a drug and started feeling better. I decided to take my best girl out on a date Jeanette. I would go to Madison Square Garden to see the Muppets Show, I bought her a nice outfit with a nice little hat, and she looked like she lived on 5th Avenue. I just spent some serious money on her, we were going to have great time together and to top it off my little princess was going to get door to door service. That's right we took a taxi from the Bronx to MSG. I was very happy for her because she was enjoying the show and she jumped up and down with happiness. I inside felt like a real responsible dad, Jeanette was high maintenance so I had 20 dollars left to take a cab back to the Bronx. When we were leaving there was a vender selling these big Muppet dolls for 12 dollars Jeanette wanted one, but I said we need the money for a cab, she start to cry and I said Ok, I bought it for her and we took the train No 2. All was going good. Anthony didn't use any drugs so I tried to rejoin our old friendship. One day I went with Anthony to bar and I would just order soda, but felt that my time without a drink was proof that it was all a hoax. A had a couple of beers and walked away. I passed the test or did I? We would go to Atlantic City a large group of us and there I drank champagne no problem. When I went to my weekly session I told them that I had found control in my drinking so I stop going. What a fool I would be.

Anthony and his wife had a full package vacation to Puerto Rico his wife could not go so she asks me if I wanted to go with him. I said yes I would love to go. I would pay her 400.00 for airfare, hotel, rental car, and a show at the Caribe Hilton, or The San Juan Hotel, I don't remember, but it was the "Le Lo Li show" the trip was for June of 1987. I was very excited I'm finally going to Puerto Rico" *me voy para Puerto rico vendiendo vasos en colores*" a song by Marvin Santiago. The last time I was there was 1962 when I was 1 years old. I started to save a little money and buy some nice shirts and pants for the trip. I was also going to meet my cousins, aunts, and uncles; we were going for 10 days. I had ask my mother like I would when I was very young *¿comó tú cre estàn los puercos de cheo.?* How do you think cheos pigs are doing? My mother said he had no pigs why do you always say that? I didn't know, it was just something that stuck with me from when I was very young. Well the day would come and we were on our way to JFK next stop San Juan. The flight was pretty long 3hours 45 minutes as we come up on the coast you could see the island it was beautiful I didn't even land and already I wanted to stay. I knew I would have a good time. We get in and as I'm walking through the terminal of course I was looking at the woman WOW why did my parents go to NY we should of kept ourselves right here. We went to get the rental car than on to the hotel the Caribbean inn in Isla Verde.

That night we would go to the show there were not many people there so we sat up in the front; it was about the *jibaros* or hicks. It was very colorful, then the girl that was dancing grabbed me and another grabbed Anthony and took us up to the stage to dance. I tell you I was redder than a tomato and I froze, she took my hands, and I just went with the flow, after we were giving 2 small bottles of Bacardi Rum. What an experience. I saw the girl later leaving the hotel and wanted to talk with her, but an older lady was with her, she would smile at me and I would say goodbye. I drank the Bacardi and I was back to the way I was when I went to rehab not thinking and lost. I went from bar to bar in San Juan and tried to fine cocaine. I didn't find any so I went back to the hotel, but got lost trying to get there. I kept finding myself in the same place every time I would try to get back to Isla Verde. Finally I made the right turn and made it to the Hotel. I had gone out by myself that evening. Anthony was a more responsible drinker than I was. He had gone back to the hotel earlier. The next day my cousin Migdalia had offered me to go Dancing with her and her husband Cheito and my other cousin Milagros. She also had a date for me her name was Wanda. Migdalia and Milagros were the Daughters of Cheo and Celia my very close aunt and uncle. The last time they saw me I was a baby so they wanted to see me. They were much older than me maybe 7-10 years older. I accepted there invitation. We would go to the Palladium in Rio Piedras. It cost 25 dollars to get into the club. That was kind of steep for me, because I didn't have much money left after my long night out in San Juan. My cousin told men not to worry, Cheito her husband was paying. We just want to see you she said, In Puerto Rico the custom is for whoever invites pays. The drinks were included in the 25 dollar entrance fee. The 2 groups that played were *Bobby Valintin and Conjunto Quesqueya.* "El Hombre de el soltero". I danced allot of meringue and salsa. Both bands were great and my date was also great. We hit it off quick, since I was a little crazy with my humor and she just getting separated from her husband, it was just the perfect time for us to meet. Of course I respected her and I watched what I said. We danced meringue, salsa, and whatever I could do to make her laugh. Laughter is always the right approach to making any woman enjoy her evening with you. I wasn't acting like a fool just being fun. I was loose and I let her know that having fun is what's important to me; especially when both of us were coming out of bad relationships.

We would meet again and spend time together one of my best days with her was when we went to the beach in *catano. Palo seco* I think. My experience with her was way different then the Nuryorican woman I grew up with. She spoke Spanish and English very well and was Educated. You could get more romantic in Puerto Rico than in NY, in my opinion. I never wanted that day to end. Sometimes moments become seconds when you are enjoying yourself.

At the moment I would off said yes if she asked me to stay, and would off bought Jeanette with me. I was trying to escape my past so much. I never wanted to go back to NY. I felt as I was living in hell when there. I went on the next day to visit family in Trujillo Alto we had to drive up a mountain to get there and you would not have any railings going up the hill. I met my uncle Otillio and Aunt Margo, and his daughters my cousins Luz Esperanza y Sandra and I can't remember the rest. We had a great time everybody laughed at my Spanish, but what the hell! It was family and I was on cloud nine from all the great things that were happening to me. Most of them were older than me so they would say I was a baby the last time they saw me. I tried to reach Wanda, but she said the time we had was great, but she was in the middle of a Divorce and still wasn't sure. I said ok and thanked her for the great time we spend together. I was a little sad, but sometimes life situations are more for the moment or an awakening, then long term. We must keep an open mind. I did know one thing: I just wanted woman from the Puerto Rico.

7 days had gone by and our hotel stay was up. We would stay with Anthony family in Caguas for the final 3 days. Several days later I would meet the Vargas family, when my cousin invited me to a party. Leon, Ana, and their daughter Terisita Vargas, and her husband Andy and their son Andres, Leon and Ana parents of Pepo who was married to my cousin Milagros, but Milagros and Pepo were both divorced. The Vargas family and my cousin Milagros, and her parents uncle Cheo and aunt Celia were very close and even though Pepo and Milagros were not together Pepo's parents Leon an Ana kept attending any functions that Celia was doing. The parties at Celia's house were always the best. She lived in Cupey Puerto Rico. I would get along with Leon the dad right away. The Vargas were a small business family who were famous for their plumbing replacing parts" *Ferriterria Vargas"* they were also into real-estate. Leon the Dad was one of the nicest people I would ever know. This guy was very easy to talk to. When young he worked as a firefighter on the base and took advantage of a plumbing course that he took. That was his ticket to becoming a business success, one of the positives of the US being in Puerto Rico. Leon also talked good English so we were able to communicate well, we would have a great relationship for many years.

Alcohol was in every activity in Puerto Rico so my drinking just got even worse, but I was able to maintain and stay away from the cocaine which is what really made me wild. The trip would come to an end, and while the plane was taking off I was writing a letter to Wanda. You see, I know what she told me, but some woman needs a second shot before you walk away. Just in case they felt you didn't want them. I would mail it as soon as we got home and she responded but the answer was still the same so I let it go. I am not possessive, once I get the picture I'm out.

Chapter 5

I would tell everybody about my experience and when I got my 2nd paycheck I bought another plane ticket to Puerto Rico for Christmas. They told me that Christmas was the best time to be there so I was going. I went back to the cocaine and started smoking crack again. I was again living in hell. My mother would take care of Jeanette and Marisa would pick her up on weekends and sometimes stay weekly with her. I started to miss time from my job and didn't do my work, but never was in trouble because my foreman really liked me and was trying to look out for me. I started looking at going into the navy, but I needed a high school diploma. I had already got my discharge from the National Guard. So I took GED classes so I could get the hell out of here and maybe talk my wife into going with me. When I took my GED test I felt as I passed it, and was making my planes to join the Navy. I got my scores and I failed, a few days later I got my divorce papers. I said: what the hell! I will die on the streets of New York like the junkie I am. How dark the life of a lost soul could be. Obstacles would be my only guarantee in life. I would jump hurdle after hurdle, and always land on my face,

In September 1987 Leon, and Ana, Teresita, and son Andres, along with my cousin Milagros were on vacation in NY. They called me and told me where we can meet. I was very happy to see them and without even thinking about it I invited Teresita to my house to meet my daughter along with my cousin Milagros. I asked them if they wanted to go dancing in New York they said yes. After they met my daughter and Milagros saw her aunt my mom Angelina. I brought them back to where they were and had a few drinks with Leon. My friend Anthony told me let's take them out, but I then said no forget it. I knew myself if I would taken 1 hit of cocaine while with those ladies my family in Puerto Rico would be angry at me and I did not want to lose the only thing I had left, that accepted me. So I stood them up, I got an angry response from them, but it was better then what it could have been.

When I snorted cocaine or smoked crack I was really different and I would be out of control. That's why I would stay away from my family when I was using. I would rather sleep in hallways and the streets before hurting anyone in my family. I would suffer a lot in that life, come November, I was again losing my mind and I would go back to rehab Gracie Square hospital. They told me welcome back are you ready to work the program this time? I said yes. I would spend another 7 days in rehab. I was told that I should cancel my trip to Puerto Rico because the temptation of alcohol would be too much for me to withstand. I said no way in hell I am going to my trip to Puerto Rico. I just will have to say no to alcohol when they offer it to me. Hahahahahahaha how ignorant I was.

I would go to Puerto Rico and by 5pm at Celias house where I was staying, I was reading the Big Book of alcoholics Anonymous with a rum and coke in my hand. It was December of 1987, I said I will stop when I get back to NY, but I should not offend anyone and drink what they offer me. The alcoholic mind is certainly insane. It continues to pour down alcohol expecting a different result all the time which is pure insanity. I went to allot of parties with the Vargas family and Milagros. I was having the time of my life. However I was killing myself slowly. I remember in one house party everybody made a circle and would share something. I have no idea why I said this; but when it was my turn I said, I will one day come live amongst my people and will have a great life with them. I would leave Puerto Rico in the New Year of1988 the year that God would change my surroundings.

I was getting closer towards my hope and dreams. My drugs and alcoholic life was getting worse and worse my job was also being threatened, I was borrowing money from Drug dealers and loan sharks that were dangerous. On payday I was trying to hide from certain people because I could not pay them all. I was worrying that I would have to fight these guys in my Job. I remember one night I had to run around and hide all over the school because people were looking for me. I would spend numerous hours in crack houses around the Bronx getting high. My family felt as it would be a matter of time that they would get a call from the police. I even forgot the love I had for Jeanette. At night when going to sleep, I started saying Hail Mary's continuous without stopping until I would fall asleep.

My mother had setup an appointment with this spiritual kid who was only 15, but my mother felt something strong about him. He came over to my home, and we talked about my life and problem. I told him that God was not responding to me that I was just being punished for being a bad person. That I would die young, I already accepted it. He told me No. that is not true. God has you on a path that will surprise you later just hold on and have faith. I remember in 1987 I went to see a palm reader who gave me a life reading and she said that it is bad now, but then opened her eyes like she saw something great and said it will get much better later. I was looking for answers, because I was really getting sick in tired of being sick and tired. I would at time try to read the big book of alcoholics anonymous, but would not go to meetings; I already have been to rehab twice. Where was the miracle? Where was my reprieve? I was embarrassed and ashamed of myself. I just wanted someone to put me out of my misery. I would go to the most dangerous places to get high, but would always leave untouched. One day while getting high with some people I saw a girl go into convulsion from the crack cocaine and it scared the living shit out of me. The others instead of helping her went through her pockets to see if she had any money. I just sat there with my eyes open in shock. I was no different than them, but for some reason I was able to see what they couldn't, the insanity we were going through. Crack was a very bad drug when used and when the girl came too all she wanted was another hit of crack.

I remember one time a well dressed man with a girl coming to buy some crack and within 1 hour he looked crazy and was asking for more. Why would I spend hours just observing this? I had no idea. I would just sit on the floor in a corner and couldn't move. I once looked out the window and saw a parade of cops coming to bust the place and I got up and ran out the back door and got away.

One day while working pulling garbage on the fifth floor, there was pictures of Spain, Greece, Italy, and I said to the young lady working there, that I will visit those countries one day. Why did I say that, I again have no idea? I would say things that would not make sense to me. In late November my Daughter would change everything for me and for her. I was in my room just thinking about how can I change things around so here come Jeanette with a newspaper in her hand. She was playing with it then was going to put it in her mouth. I said Jeanette give me that. It was Sunday and it was the classified ads. I saw US. Navy looking for Merchant Marine to work aboard Naval Vessels traveling around the world no experience is needed. There was a phone Number listed. So first thing Monday morning I called and they told me to report to the Unemployment Office in journal Sq. New Jersey. I ask if I needed a High School Diploma. They said no it's not needed, thanks Ronald Reagan for building up the military so much they were expanding their civilian forces to take care of naval needs all over the world.

When I went for the interview there were allot of people on line for the same Job. I had over herd that the starting salary was $10.000 dollars a year. I said hell no I make 17,000 a year at Hostos. I was thinking about leaving, "Here It goes", this white boy from I don't even know from where, He Grabs me and said "don't leave you will make more money than that "stay he says". Thank God I closed my eyes to his color and said ok I'll stay. I was hired on the spot. I had a clean record no felonies. I was able to get clearance. God sure knows how to put a plan together I could not have done it any better. I was giving a date to take a physical at the Military ocean terminal Bayonne New Jersey. I would work for The Dept of the Navy, Military Sealift Command Atlantic. The mission was to replenish military naval Ships at sea.

The ship had a Civilian Captain, civilian mariners, and a small naval detachment on board. I took my physical and passed it then went on to firefighting school in earl New Jersey, well I was going to the Navy after all, but, as a civilian that would pay me overtime when working after 5pm and on weekends, better deal. I was giving my first ship the USNS Sirius AFS-8 I would fly to Alicante Spain to meet the ship along with a few others. I was going to the *madre patria españa*. How do you go from one day sitting in a crack house to a magical trip to Spain, and going to work on the ocean? I knew now that my life was special and that I was here to do something for God. I remember the pictures I would draw when young it was a ship and a house. The most difficult moment I would have to encounter, was saying goodbye to Jeanette. I told her that daddy would get better and we were going to have a better life in another city, I will be back for you, and while I was hugging her, in my mind I said thank you for saving my life. I would make an allotment of 200 dollars a month in my mother's name, for Jeanette and also gave her health Insurance and all my life Insurance. I would not go out for anything. I locked ` myself up in the house until the day of my flight.

I arrived at JFK at 4 pm to meet up with the other mariners that were going to Spain like the good sailors we were, we had a few drinks. We boarded the plane and on our way for 6hours across the Atlantic to visit the first conquerors of the Caribbean. I was going to visit the Real Spanish speaking people and I couldn't wait to get there. I slept for most off the flight since it was a night flight. We would get to Madrid and it was already morning, because Europe is six hours ahead. The currency was pesetas and it wasn't hard for me and the other Puerto Ricans that were with me to get around, because we all spoke Spanish. The first Spaniard that I talked to gave me the impression that she had something in her mouth? What's Up here they talk so funny. I thought they had big tongues. They also knew we were Puerto Rican, because of the way we spoke Spanish. Something likes that that is exactly how it sounded to me. We went on to our connecting flight and landed in Alicante. We jump into a cab, I tell the guy" *llevame al balco Americano de navy por favor.* [Take me to the American navy ship please] The cab driver very nicely told me you speak Spanish? I said yes. He started telling me off all the hot spots to go to.

I reported to the Ship and got squared away. I went back to the cab and hung out in Alicante that night. It was a beautiful place the ceramic and cobblestone streets, old style cement houses, buildings, and small cars. It looked just like old San Juan Puerto Rico. I walked into a bar and started talking with the people and met a very nice lady. We drank wine and ate tapas real tapas. Tapas are small food like sardines, Cheese, ham, shrimp with the heads on, stuff like that. The other mariners were also there and we all had a great time. We took pictures with the Spanish ladies so we could get our friends back home jealous. Some of the sailors were married but didn't care. I was a free agent. I could do whatever, because I was single. The Moroccan women were beautiful; they were fair skinned with dark hair just the way I like it. They were a lot of Moroccans living in Spain. At one time the Moroccans conquered Spain they were the moors.

I would experience Moorish castles that were built 100s of years ago, but I would get drunk and walk back to the ship the same way when I was in America. The worse hangover in the world is wine. I was almost late for my first day of work. Thanks to one of my new friends who woke me up at 0600, that's 6 am. We needed to be on deck at 6.30 am. I was in the Steward Department. The job was to maintain the officers quarters and work in the kitchen or Mess Hall. I didn't care, it was a job and I got out of NY and was traveling to countries I could not even dream of seeing.

The mess hall was manned by mostly Puerto Ricans and African Americans. We had Rice and chicken Puerto Rican style on the menu. We were a union under SIU Seafarers International Union. We had a better menu then the navy's menu. What the captain ate we ate. However when you worked in the galley, you ate better then everybody anyway.

The ship would get under way on to sea. I went out on deck to see the ocean and as we left the seagulls were following us out to sea. I felt as I was leaving the world and everything behind. A new me would emerge as I thanked God for this wonderful voyage I was on. We would right away go to work and the Aircraft carrier John F Kennedy came along side for supplies. We would work all day and in the evening settle in. There is nothing more spectacular than watching the sun come down while at sea. At night it's very dark if the moon is not full and you could see all the stars, Planets, the universe, boy! How grateful I would be to experience such beauty. I felt like my past life was a million years away and that I would find the true meaning of gratitude for I was free.

Other than my galley job I had another. I was assigned to Unrep team Bravo. The call was this. "The time is 0500 flight, Quarters, flight Quarters all Flight Quarters all Flight Quarters personal mann the flight deck." My job was to fight any fire that would occur from a helicopter crash. The Navy personal would direct and pilot the helicopter. We also were sending cargo to other ships using the helicopter. We would place cargo in large nets, than we attached a large pole with an open round end at the end. The helicopter would drop down a little towards the deck enough where we could reach, and we then hand over the pole to someone who would grab it and hook it to the bottom of the helicopter. They would take it and drop it on the receiving ship; it was dangerous, but very exciting to watch. On the side of the ship we had the receiving ship alongside. We setup a highline tension cable to the other ship hook then sling on a pallet with cargo and swing it across to the other ship. There would be more ships lined up waiting their turn, or we have ships on both sides. The job brought us at least 32 hours of overtime minimum, I guess that's what that guy meant when he told me I would make more money.

They were times we have 92 hours of overtime and our checks. My pay was almost 1700 dollars every two weeks. Though I had a small salary I made at least 3000 a month back then in 88, 89. Naples Italy would be a port I remember on that trip. I would drink more wine. I did not speak Italian, but they understood my Spanish, because it's almost the same. They had some very nice suits so I brought me a couple and got my daughter some Italian ware also. Naples Italy was pure New York. The apartment building looked the same as those in the Bronx. You would see the laundry hanging out the windows drying. We would go on to Augusta Bay Sicily, next and that was also the same, but the people were different. Very country and family oriented. I did not like the pizza and there was not much to do there. The clothes and perfumes were always good so I got my mother some things and went back to the ship. After watching the movie Godfather, and Godfather2, I did not want to mess around in Sicily. So when it came to Italy I would walk very easy. Malaga Spain was a killer!! boy was that place party city. We were there for 11 days the party place was a 15 dollar cab ride to *torremolinos*, a vacation spot for Europeans, along with a strip mall of British Pubs. Boy! Can those Britts drink. The discos didn't start till 12 midnight. By then I would be drunk like a skunk, but would force myself to hang out. I would go around the corner and vomit from so much alcohol, the change of scenery was not changing me I was still drinking allot. I wasn't using any cocaine, because I didn't find any. I tried dancing, but was so drunk that I fall down and made a fool out of myself, my body was wearing down. We left and went to Rota Spain to pick up some cars and steam back to Norfolk.

Rota Spain was a great place to get your personal things taken care off. It was the United States Naval station which meant post office, navy exchange, and commissary. They had some nice bars outside, but I learned not to go out till 10 pm or 11. The Eden club was the hot spot. Mostly locals, but a lot of navy who were stationed there, you also had Shorty's, A Spanish style fast food restaurant that made the best fried rice for 500 pesetas or 5 bucks. They also had these gypsies, trying to sell us hashish, a drug that you smoked, that wasn't me. However I did try it and was paranoid the whole time. So I decided to stay away from it. I was a coke head that was my drug of choice.

We left Rota and started our trip to Norfolk Virginia. Norfolk was new to me so I started asking question about where to go and what to do. People told me about the clubs and all. My first club was Knickerbockers. That was the club back in 89 it was more like a rock place, across the street they had the fox trap which was R&B. My number 1 club was trade winds yes the club on the base. Trade-winds would get packed it would close at

12 midnight, and then you would go to Knickerbockers, Gary's, or the fox trap. The clubs stop serving alcohol at 1:30 am. That really sucked if you were me. I was use to drinking into the next day.

I met a new girl in Norfolk her Name was Gisele a Panamanian girl who married a sailor in Panama, but they just have broken up. They is something about me always meeting divorced woman. She spoke more Spanish then English so we got along great. I spoke Spanish, and I was wild and she like that, however this would not be your regular faithful relationship we were just friends. When we got together we enjoyed each other's company.

We go out to eat then go dancing. I would make her laugh with my crazy self. I treated her very well. I felt sorry for her she was really hurt over her husband leaving her in a foreign country for he did bring her to Norfolk from Panama. In Hampton Roads divorce is constant along with a large number foreign woman. She was great to be with. However I did not like Hampton roads to much so I asked to be paid off the ship when we arrive at the shipyard. I went home to New York and went to see my daughter and family and spent some time with them. Marisa and her family came over to greet me I had sent letters to her sister Miosotis, letting her know how I was doing. My feelings about Marisa had change and I saw myself better off staying single. I wanted to enjoy dating different woman everywhere I went. I decided to just be a host and not try to persuade Marisa into another relationship.

A week later I went to the base in New Jersey. I was sent back to Spain to meet the USNS Regal another cargo ship. I would fly to Cartagena Spain. That was a drug city if you ever saw one. I would find cocaine there and used it. I would find crack cocaine in Spain and will get high with Spanish crack heads. Oh my God, how a junkie would find his dosage where ever he is. One night I was giving heroin by mistake and I snort it like cocaine and almost overdosed. I was taken to the ship by several of my shipmates and they kept me awake. I was lucky that I didn't overdose. We left and I would escape another episode with cocaine and almost an overdose from heroin. We went to Malaga Spain my favorite port and I would do the same as I did when I was there before, drink, drink, and drink. I remember dancing with a lady, I tried to dip her and fell right on top of her, hurting her pretty bad. I was told to leave. The next morning in the mess hall I was the talk of the morning they found what I did funny so I made everybody's day with my antics. We go to Palma De Mollorca Spain that was a beautiful port, I went to a show in a castle and had Paella, and Sangria it was very nice and I had a good time. The drifters were performing I gave myself a treat and managed to hold up and not get wild like in the past. However my drinking would just get worse and I lost control. The only thing helping me was, a large percentage of mariners got drunk in port, as long as you showed up for work all was good. In Europe you could drink anytime, anywhere, anyplace whenever you get ready.

They don't waste a lot of time trying to tell you what to do, if you get in trouble you are screwed, it's that simple. The European people to me were nice people to be around they demanded respect, but they would respect you also. They believed in family time so you would have 2-4 hours of family time during the day all the stores would close. The morals were old, but not hypocrite like hear in America. They didn't have many rules when coming to having fun they were very liberal with life.

We would shove off back to Norfolk; the ship was going to the shipyard. After spending some time in Norfolk and going to visit my family in New York. I would fly back to Europe This time I was going to the USNS John, Lenthall, a fuel tanker, I was going to sleep on tons of fuel. This was one of the newest ships of MSC. I met the ship in Catania Sicily. That flight was nothing but drinking from the time I got on the plane till the time I got off. The Stewardess got so tiered of me calling for another drink she just gave me a bunch of small liquor bottles. When I got to Rome I had an 8 hour layover. So I decided to go to the coliseum. I left the airport and purchased a bus ticket, and on I went to the coliseum. I was so drunk that when they said coliseum, I looked quickly said ahhh!! And went back to sleep on the bus, and then went back to the airport. What a waste!! I took my connecting flight and went on to Sicily. The tanker spent more days at sea than in port. I was able to clean out my system eat healthy, exercise, and get myself together.

We stop in Palma De Mollorca Spain; this was almost my last night alive. I decided to go alone to Playa De Palma pretty far away from the ship. I went to a real nice Disco. There was this beautiful girl singing and I wanted her badly. So I invited her to my table to drink some champagne. She would come over with another girl and the lead singer. We talked, and were having a real good time, the lead singer wasn't going to let me get her, I noticed it quick. I introduced myself as an entertainment manager looking for talent in Europe to take back to the states. The story sounded so good I believed it myself. It caused me to continue to feed the enthused entertainers with so much Bullshit they even sang a song for me. However I was not getting the girl and I was becoming inpatient. I gave up and decided it was just a waste of time to continue. I asked for my bill and when I received it I got angry. I said very loud I wasn't paying for this shit and called them a bunch of fucking Spanish fagots!! I screamed!!! I'm Puerto Rican I kick all your asses. They ask me to leave and I did, thinking I got over on not paying the bill. I walked outside, some guys walked towards me; in my mind I said "this is it". I threw a punch at one of them and missed and they started beating me. I held my hands up to protect my face and head.

Then with a stick or something someone hit me right in the face and knocked out my front teeth. I fell to the floor like a boxer who was just knocked out, as they kicked me and stomped me I said in my mind please finish me off. I hear a police car show up and he yelled," hey stop that," They stopped and just like nothing, I got up and slowly walked to a cab and said, take me to the American ship as blood was pouring down my shirt. He took me to the police station and they very nicely ask me if I wanted to go to the hospital? I said no take me to the ship please. I went to the ship and they fixed me up, 2 hours later I went back to another bar, this time closer to the ship.

I hit a bottom so low, that I myself didn't understand how I let myself get so bad.

I flew back to the United States and everybody was looking at me on the flight. I had bruises, and my front teeth were knocked out. I healed and fixed my front teeth, which cost me some serious money along with insurance. I don't know what hurt more the price for new front teeth or the knockout punch I got.

I went back to the USNS Sirius right before it left for Spain, so for the first time I traveled to Europe by ship instead of plane. I would switch from Steward Dept to Deck dept. I was in line to control my own destiny. In the deck dept, when you have the sea time you can upgrade and could go all the way to Captain. Many Captains started just like me. Plus I was making more money, But I was also spending allot. I started borrowing money from people who would lend for interest. Yes' it was like being at Hostos College all over again. Little by little I played myself right into what I ran away from, giving away my money on payday. I would go through a whole trip and not have any money when I returned to the states. I would ride the USNS Sirius for 1 year and was written up 2 times for being late. One time in Rota Spain I was a club and that night the ship was leaving at 5 am. I was talking with this beautiful Moroccan woman. I told her I had to leave, but I would be back. I go to the ship and Tony Torres my boss was at the gangway. I tell him, Hey Tony I got this hot ass chick tell the captain to delay the trip I will be finished in 2 hours. He looked at me like I was crazy and told me, get your ass below before I fire you right here.

Chapter 6

I flew to Cagliari, Sardinia to meet the USNS Truckee an old tanker on its last deployment. This ship was really wild a lot of people would get in trouble on this ship. I also met a lady who I liked very much. Her name was lea she was half Moroccan and half French she was beautiful I met her In Gaeta Italy. We were in port for 1 week she was awesome. We met several times but shipboard life means quick relationships than off to sea. The great thing about this job is, it would pause your life, because you were always going to Sea so if you where planning on making a mistake you would be saved. I would recuperate at Sea and think. I would sit on the stern of the ship which is the back, when I was not working. The propellers turning and driving us forward; and my mind turning also with thoughts of where will I wind up? I did a lot of talking to God while sitting there. When at Sea there is nothing man made just miles of ocean and sky so you are really in the house of God. People would go to the stern to smoke or reflect like myself. I would quiet down and talk to God within. I wasn't like these phonies always trying to pray in front of people so they could say he is religious, I would hide my religious beliefs. My spirituality was between me and God no one else and that was the way I felt about religion, or Spirituality. Some things were still turning in my mind from when I was in rehab. I just wasn't practicing what I was taught.

I was disciplined twice for being late, or for not doing my job. My position as a mariner was in jeopardy. I was starting to worry about what I will do if I lost my job. Will my fate be living on the streets like a bum with nothing to live for? My fear of seeing the end of Tyrone was near; I would die young from a gunshot wound or an overdose of drugs. How dark was my life for I had no answer to my problem. My prayers will not reach God and my continuance of addiction was growing like an incurable cancer. I was overly matched and was losing the game of the drug and alcoholic life I was living.

The ship was on its way back to Norfolk. While steaming through the Mediterranean, Iraq had invaded Kuwait and we were told to turn around and head for the Eastern Mediterranean. The United States would get involved and we were diverted in order to help. We were the on station tanker while Navy war ships traveled thru the Suez Canal. We would fuel the ships before going through the Suez Canal. It felt good to be part of that oncoming war. The President in Charge was George H. W. Bush (Dad). It was called Operation Desert Shield. We were making some good money, because we were working allot of overtime fueling ships and receiving fuel. The Mediterranean was a madhouse of naval war ships racing towards the Suez Canal. I never saw so many War ships, Marines, artillery; this was really cooking up to be a war. The US built up for 6 months sending troops. Everything was on its way to the Middle East. That would be the new home. I would go there another time. The Middle East wasn't ready for Tyrone. We were relieved by another ship and steamed on home.

I then would be assigned to The USNS Mohawk a Sea going tug boat. We were towing targets for naval war ships practicing shooting; in Florida we would visit Key West Florida. I saw the house of the famous writer Earnest Hemmingway, and walked up and down Duvall Street where drinking was the only thing to do. I would find Duvall as a heaven for alcoholics for the alcohol was everywhere you walked. Our next port would be Cape Canaveral, it was November or December of 1990, I was drunk in public and was arrested. I was put in a cell and all I remember was me screaming. I yelled "let me out" I don't like in here" the police tried to shut me up, but they couldn't. I eventually went to sleep. I woke up the next day and felt terrible. I was worrying about losing my Job behind this. The Captain came to get me and they let me go. On the Car ride back, I didn't say a word out of fear the Captain would go off on me. I asked for a transfer to go back to Europe. I got it. I would then be assigned to The Sea going tug boat USNS Apache. This would be my last ship as a drunk.

I flew to Norfolk and reported to the ship. We would get underway in Feb, 1991. Operation Desert storm already took place and it was a success. We were in operation desert shortie. Our mission was to tow ships or assist any ship that was disabled. Our first job was to recover a ship that was dead in the water half way to Europe. When we got there the swells were pretty bad so trying to get close enough to shoot a shot line up to the bow of the ship was hard. The winds were not letting us do that. I and others believed that if they threw down to us the messenger which was a line to retrieve a cable, it would be easier. Well the big ship ran into us and almost sunk us. The Captain was still able to retrieve the dead in the water ship. [Or the Crew] My eyes were wide open as the monster roll on roll off ship collided with our little one. I quickly believed that I would have my little titanic ending for it was February in the Atlantic, and the water was cold. We would both crawl into Lisbon Portugal for 1-2 months in the shipyard. I loved it! That was a very nice port.

The people did not speak Spanish, they spoke Portuguese, but they understood Spanish, so I was able to get around. Of course when staying that long you need a Lady to keep you company, so I found one. Even though! I was a big womanizer, I gave them the respect they deserve no matter what they were bad, good, decent, even bitches. I never forced a woman to do anything with me. I was the type of person that if you didn't want me somebody else will. So there was no reason for me to mistreat any woman, a matter of fact! When going to ports

I was in before, some of the woman was looking for me. I gave them money treated them to Restaurants, bought them clothes, even pay their bills. Same thing you do when you are married, the only difference is you know it's temporary, and you don't get to close, so, No hard feelings.

The dream of having a wife that loves you is always better, but, I wasn't going to get serious with a woman knowing I was a worthless piece of crap and could not make her happy, so I settled for what I was getting. That is what makes me feel so good about myself, I was honest with myself. I wasn't the selfish kind of guy who would bring in some poor girl into a horrible relationship. I learned my lesson with Marisa. If you're not ready to make a woman happy, leave her alone.

The ship would get repaired and Stationed in Rota Spain. In April 1991, Rota was a mad house. Ships were coming back from the war. They were stopping in Rota before going to Norfolk. The port was packed with sailors and party, party, party, all the clubs were filled, and women were all around. "Or the vultures were out". I had found cocaine in Rota, where I could go whenever I needed some. I also found me a couple of nice lady's to spend the time with. One American and one Moroccan, I would switch off whenever I wanted. Until the American one busted me at Paul's a club outside the base kissing with the Moroccan one at the bar.

I remember the next day renting a car and driving to Seville, were I got drunk and wanted some cocaine. I found this club and met some people and they sold me some, but all it did was knock me out and they robbed me. When I woke up the only thing I was mad about was, they took my fifth of rum, "Mother Fuckers" This is real nutso of me. While sitting in my car angry, a man walked up to me and asks if I could take him to the hospital. I said come on. I took him to the hospital. When inside I said my name, and that I was a doctor. "I yelled" this man needed assistance right away. I did it so good that they actually believed that I was a doctor. The man got immediate attention. They took care of him and He told me thank you. I said goodbye and left. As I walked away he looked at me like I was crazy, I was. I would drive like a mad man back to Rota almost 100 miles an hour, in Europe you could drive any Speed you want. I believe I was starting to really lose my mind after that one. While speeding back like a man on a death wish I started to analyze what I finished doing. I said I'm gone. I would sleep and wake up and brush it off and say I was just high! I am alright.

Time passed and for several days I would walk to the beach, and just look at the water, and wonder when is this going to be over. My life had become a circus of fools and nuts. I was in prison not physically, but mentally, one cannot be free if his mind is clouded with addictions. I would be owned by the puppet master, and my strings would be pulled whenever I tried to break free. One night I had the Midnight to-8am watch. I was pretty drunk and when morning had arrived, as I drank while on the gangway. I stormed into the mess hall "screaming and yelling" the captains herd me. He told me to meet him in his office. I went up see him He said Garcia; I am recommending that you go home and are removed from your position. Termination; However I believe your problem is more alcohol then just you. So I will also recommend Rehabilitation. If you go and are successful you will not lose your Job. What could I say he gave me a choice this would be my 3rd trip to Rehab, but this time instead of 7 days it was 28days.

I flew back to where I started NY. My dad in disgust of me! Except my Mom she always was looking for excuses why we were the way we were. My dad was Bruto conjo "stupid" that was my other name. I remember when young, when my dad was angry, he would bend his tongue and slide his belt off his paints like Zorro. The belt looked like it had a lubricant, because he had no problem sliding that belt off his trousers.

Well I had let everybody down even Jeanette my little girl. Well! Before one goes to rehab one must get high one more time. I had about 2,000 dollars on me and went to orchard Beach in the Bronx. I bought some cocaine and some readymade crack, there was a DJ on Sundays, and so I went to party and met a couple of girls who had their own place. We get high for a couple of days. We were in a tall building on the 17th floor. As we were passing the drugs around I came out and said or a voice said," why are we killing ourselves like this"? The girls looked at me like I was crazy. I got up walked to the window and thought of jumping out and ending the whole thing, but I got very nervous and ran out the apartment. I ran down the stairs in frenzy and when I got outside I starting yelling for help, please help me 'I yelled! as I ran down a cab. One stopped, and took me to the same hospital I was born in Jacobi. When I got there I ran inside the emergency room yelling I'm dying please help me" the doctor said sir your alright have a seat and relax. I did then when I was called I told the nurse I'm supposed to report to rehab in a few days. I should go home, when I got home I looked at my daughter and said you almost lost your daddy tonight I laid down in my bed and my daughter sat and watched me, that would be the last time I would drink and drug. I was 30 years old.

The date was June 2, 1991. But I will still have a tremendous obstacle ahead 28 days in a Rehab. The next day I went to the base in New Jersey and reported to CEAP Civilian Employee Assistance Program. I talked to a councilor, and I could off talk myself out of it, but I knew I needed to go. I would go to Smithers, a rehab that once belonged to a millionaire he donated it to a hospital in Manhattan and it was converted into a Rehab for alcohol &drug abuse. It was on Manhattan upper East Side 90th Street I block away from central Park. I would meet the famous Mary Quill a counselor I would never forget. Till today she is the only counselor I remember. I remember her asking me if I ever wanted to commit Suicide. I answered no "I love myself" after thinking about it, and noticing the look she gave me. I said' if I'm here I guess I might be a little insane.

I started treatment and in the beginning I just sat, watched, and had an attitude. I didn't participate much because after a few days of being sober, we believe we can go and try to conquer alcohol again. I felt if I could just act like I'm ok I could leave and get on another ship. Europe was my hiding spot. I would spend from December 88, to-May, 91 in European countries. I would write allot in rehab, we were told to write an inventory of our past lives. I did and had almost 9 pages written and still had more to write. The first 2 weeks I was just getting by. On the third week there was a reunion of past patients, like an alumni, they would come and share with the patients how their lives were going. That day came and like always I sat around and listen, but did not participate. I herd of how their lives had gotten better without the drinking and drugs. How they were going on vacations with their families etc. That killed me, because is what I wanted to have to. That night there was a meeting. I had to be there they would share a little about themselves and would ask us to share also. I got up and raised my hand, with a lump in my throat I said, "Please give me what you have" I fell to pieces and cried. I cried till almost midnight it's like my life and my mind went all the way back to the beginning when I was in the first grade getting embarrassed by the nun, and my gang life, my hate, my resentment, everything all at once. My mind would become a television set and just replay it all, it is like the Hand of God touched me and allowed me to be humble. I felt no more hate only guilt of being who I was and how much I wanted to tell everybody I was sorry for what I have done to them and myself. I only wanted to be loved. That was a great spiritual experience I had, and my belief of a God was confirmed he herd and answered my prayer; thank you God.

My last 2 weeks was great I was starting to participating, along with reading the basic text the Big Book of AA. I would do more than read it; I would become a student of the book. I had to learn to live life without alcohol. I learned I suffered from a hopeless state of the mind and the body, that when the thought of alcohol came to mind, I would drink and I would jump start a craving for alcohol that was uncontrollable for me to fight. I needed a spiritual experience!! It's what I needed in order to beat the disease. I would need to learn a new way of thinking and through a higher power I could win this battle. The most important attitude I took was? I was doing it for me. I no longer was doing it for my daughter, or anyone, I was doing it for me. So I can survive. My family would benefit better that way.

I left the rehab and went to an alcohol support group meeting in Manhattan the workshop. I would pick my first sponsor as soon as I got there. He was a young white kid and had some good knowledge of the program. I saw everyone as the same. I only wanted to get better and beat the problem by using the program, he would be temporary until I would find someone in the Bronx he did a great job helping me and I ask God to bless him. When coming to race, drugs and alcohol is an equal opportunity employer.

Chapter 7

I would begin my new journey; I would have to wait 2more months before going back to work, because of all my suspensions. I took a job driving a van picking up and dropping off mentally challenged people, so I can have some money. I called Giselle and asked her if she wanted to come to NY, she said yes. I bought her a plane ticket and offered her stay with me. I told her everything about me and what I was going to do. I asked her if she wanted to continue our relationship. She said she would think about it. While the days went by I noticed she didn't get along with my daughter, my daughter did not like her neither. Strike 1, I also told her things would have to change, she didn't want to strike 2, I told her that things will get better, I will buy a house and we could have a better life and that I would become faithful to her, no more messing around she would be my queen. We spend 10 days together in New York and after she went back to Norfolk. She didn't answer my calls, so I left her alone. I met my new sponsor. He was on ex heroin addict and radical, but he had a strong Knowledge of the 12 steps. We start working the 12 steps together. The 12 steps are powerful program of action, which is ego deflating and brings allot of change into your character. Here is how they work, 1-3 Acceptance, open mind, and willingness. 4-9 was inventory of oneself, sharing it with God and someone else, humility, restitution, 10-12, continuing to take inventory of oneself meditation and spirituality, passing the message to another, and a higher power, It did not matter what God it was, as long as you accepted it to be greater than yourself. That was the program as I learned it in the 12 steps.

My sponsor would start by telling me who to listen to and hangout with, he became my big brother and I would become a new born baby, trying to learn. I had to trust in him. I would go to 12 step study groups, and would listen to people share about their experience, strength, and hope; I give no input, because I did not have anything to give. I just listened. I was starting life over again and I had to change my old form of thinking into a new one just like a business that dumps its old stock and fills his shelves with new stock.

I always believed what happen to me in the hospital was a spiritual awakening, that I already did these steps, but my sponsor wanted me to do them again and I did. Step In three I was willing to do whatever to get sober no procrastination. We read the book together and I will call him every night and we would talk about spirituality. He was the perfect sponsor for me. I had no problem with God so talking spiritually was something I accepted. I wanted sobriety bad. I was staying sober and finding a power in this program, it was working. People were noticing the change in me quick. I was broke financially, but what they saw was a glow in me I never had. I wasn't talking to no one. I walked through the projects like nobody was around. I was focused on God and that's all. It turned Giselle off, she didn't like the new me, too bad, I liked the new me and was intending on keeping the new me. My suspension would come to an end. I would put together 3 months of sobriety and had a great foundation of the 12 steps. I went back to work and was assigned to the USNS Neosho. The ship was just hanging around the area and was not due to deploy. It was going to be decommissioned the following year of May of 1992. I was going to my alcohol support groups in Norfolk. There was a navy Rehab on Base and they had vans that went to meetings every night. So I would walk over to the Rehab and go to meetings with them. After every meeting I call my sponsor and talk with him about what I heard. He would give me feedback and I would obey. I tried to contact Giselle one more time and I did, we got together and she told me that she was not interested in my new way of life, but good luck to me anyway. So I than buried the relationship for good and moved on. I didn't try to pursue her because I remember my ex wife Marisa, how much she tried to change me and It didn't work so I walked away.

The holidays were coming I had 5 months of sobriety and I felt it was time I start looking for the woman who was going to be my bride. I wanted to start a family so I could bring Jeanette to live with me and also wanted to be loved by someone also. I started dating and that went south, I was not use to being with woman sober so I was back to being shy. I was too honest when I talked to them and some thought I was obnoxious. I was interviewing not dating maybe that was the problem.

The ship went to sea. We made a stop at the naval base in Puerto Rico, and there was this Puerto Rican girl who worked at the phone center. She was pretty hot and she was always arguing with her husband over the phone. So one day I said "hey if you married me you wouldn't have to argue so much". I tell her in Spanish, but not in the best way. She looked at me and I thought she was going to send me to hell!! But, she smiled, and said she loves her husband and they are trying to work things out. I tell her very nicely if you change your mind I will be back here in December. She tells me ok. I had made up my mind I wanted a Puerto Rican woman. I was already tiered of the others I had a lot of woman in my life, but there is nothing better than the love of a Puerto Rican woman especially when they come from the Island. All women are beautiful, I wanted to stick to my own kind.

So On the night of December 23rd 1991 we were traveling in circles waiting for morning to pull into the port of Puerto Rico. I look up at the Stars while on the bow of the ship that is the front.

I said . . . . "God I need a woman who I could trust". "I want a Puerto Rican woman I don't care if she has kids, and she's broke, she has to look good, but not perfect." I want to take her with me and give her a good life. "I want to buy a house and take vacations with her and the kids and sing at Christmas, along with my daughter please allow me this wish".

The next day as scheduled we went into port of Puerto Rico, I asked the mate for 4 days off he approved it, I went to my aunts Celia's house and surprised them all. I asked if I could stay with them, of course she said yes. When my cousin Milagro came home from work she asks "what you are doing here? I said the ship was in port and I got a few days off. She said tomorrow me and Teresita were going to a club to hear music. I'm going to set you up with her. I ask isn't she married to Andy, she said they have been divorced for 3 years. I felt that I was out of Terisitas league. Teresita came from an upper class business family in Puerto Rico. I come from a poor family, plus I was a recovering alcoholic with a bad past I didn't fit in. I told Milagros my concerns and she told me the last time I was here Teresitas dad took a liking to me, so don't worry and just be yourself. I said I do not drink anymore. She said Teresita doesn't Drink much neither. I said I don't drink any alcohol; I then talked to my family and told them what had happen to me. They were very proud that I had noticed that I had a drinking problem and took care of it.

Well I was not to keen on Teresita, because I asked God for a poor girl not a rich one, but the 25th of December would come and we would go to a club. Teresita looked very nice and had dyed her hair Reddish blond it looked very good on her. I was very nervous and it came to my mind again what is it with me and divorced woman. I would make her laugh when I asked the waiter to bring us some appetizers, I had asked for picadillas the waiter and Teresita both looked at me, and said what! I said "algo para picar. Something to nibble on Teresita said entremeses is what it called. So we laughed and I learned some proper Spanish. There was a very good looking girl that caught my eye. I looked and was busted by Teresita, she was angered! I said to myself wow we just met. I had forgotten I was not with a street woman I was with a decent woman that demanded respect. If you are with her in friendship or as lovers you still have to Respect. Well the club was pretty dead and my cousin wanted to go home it was 11; 30pm Terisita asked me if I wanted to continue hanging out? I said sure, so we went to the Caribe Hilton to hear music. Inside there was a disco, lobby with a band, and a coffee shop.

We decided to go to the coffee shop and spend the rest of the night talking. The waiter kept bringing coffee and we talked about ourselves, our families, our goals everything, and anything you can talk about. She liked my honesty. I did not hold back nothing they would be no surprises with me, this is me take it or leave it. We left about 430am and she took me to my aunt's house. She would drop me off about 5 am and I ask her what she was doing later? She said working at her dad business and collecting rent which is something she also did for her dad. I told her I had to go back to the base tomorrow night. So she said I will take you to the base. I said great.

Teresita comes get me the next day, and we would drive to cieba where the base was located. We stop in Fajardo, because there was a carnival and Oscar de Leon was performing. We watched and then would continue, with the trip to the base. That was a long ride, but we had fun and I noticed she was pretty cool, and maybe this could work. No matter what! Hampton Roads would have to be her new home. When we got to the pier she gave me a letter that I couldn't open till the New Year. I looked at her and gave her a hug goodbye. I saw that she wanted this new relationship to continue. So I told her that my life is in transition and my job takes me away from time to time. She said "that it would be worth the wait". I then gave her an honest kiss. I told her we were due back in on January 1st

The night before we went back into port I was waiting till midnight to read the letter. I wanted to respect her wish, so I opened the letter at exactly Midnight like she asked me to. The letter was a check for 1 million kisses. I said well it is going to take some time to spend 1 million kisses. I believe Teresita is the chosen one, the woman God has sent to me. We would go out and have great times together. The ship went in and out of Puerto Rico for a month. It all went our way. She would drive from Rio Piedras to ceiba to pick me up when the ship was in. I would go to the Navy exchange and buy myself a new wardrobe of clothes to wear every time I went out with her. The selection was not that bad at the exchange in Puerto Rico, it was better than Norfolk's navy exchange. I bought socks, shoes, pants, belt, shirt, everything was new why? Because I was new, our hangout at Night would always be The Caribe Hilton in San Juan. We would only go for dancing and hearing music no funny business.

We sit on the private beach of the Hilton and talk and get a little romantic only kissing, no harm in that. I was really learning how to love a woman better than just hit the bed do your business and see you later. There is more to a relationship then that. Allowing inner emotions to combine together is the true essence of love, and the power to stay faithful with each other. We would stay till 5 am at the beach. Then I needed to get to the base by 10 am. So Teresita, said she needed to go home and Change before she can take me. I said ok. We went to her home and she jumps in the shower and my mind is saying, is this sign? I wonder if she wants me to come inside. Hum, I said to myself if I'm a wrong I would mess up a nice thing going, if I'm right it would be great. It is like having the little angel on one side and the little devil on the other side. I said no! I will pass this is the woman I want and I could also trust her with Jeanette. I'm no longer a low budget sex scene; a cold shower when I get back to the ship would have to do.

Sometime later I asked her about it, and she said, "I was very nervous that if you would off walked in I was going to scream". I guess I made the right decision. Sobriety was starting to work for me in all aspect of my life. The ship would sail back to Norfolk and I would continue my spiritual work with my sponsor and the 12 steps. I was going to see him in late May because I wanted to celebrate my 1st sober birthday in NY. When in Norfolk, I brought a tape recorder. I would record myself singing love songs; I would talk, and make jokes, just like if she was in front of me to my future wife. I use to call it the Tyrone hour like a show. She loved it very much. All this without getting laid, it shows that I wasn't an animal after all. I was finding out that I was a good person that just wanted love, affection, laugh, and enjoy life every day.

I made plans to go to Puerto Rico, in May after I finish my tour on the ship. We were going to spend a month together, and that was going to determine our decision. I was going to stay in my aunt's house and Teresita would pick me up. I flew to San Juan and Teresita picked me up at the Airport. While taking me to my aunt's house she said how about you just stay with me? I said well the best way to learn about each other is when you live together. I also stated that we are divorced and we are in our 30s. So we both decided, I would stay with her and it was the right thing to do. Her family being Christian didn't like the idea, but it was our life not theirs. Once you have been married and divorced you are more experienced so you know what to look for. I would talk to her son Andres who was 12 years old and Leonell who was 3 years old. In the morning her father would pick me up at 7 am to go help him with his properties, He was preparing one to rent out so he needed some help. I painted and spend time with Leon Vargas and some of his workers and Friends there was Don Kekie, Napo, and Cotto, and some others I can't remember. I had a great time working with them. I was learning about Puerto Ricans from the island they were very different.

My Spanish was always being corrected. Mira Muchacho eso no se decir asi. "Son! you don't say it that way". Leon wasn't like that, because he spoke good English. This is the funny part! as I just remembered while writing this story. He sits me down and asked me, what were my plans? I said, to take your daughter and her kids to Norfolk, Then I will buy a house continue with my Job, then one day I would write a book and become successful. He looked at me and said ok, I respect your goals. It was left at that nothing else said. Leonides Vargas was the most humble person I ever knew. He never put you down or disrespected you, he always respect your wishes. The guy could of drove a Mercedes, but would drive humble cars; he was old school, came from poverty to successful business man. I learned a lot from him. I wanted to call him dad, but I was scared to do it. I was enjoying my new family.

We did a lot of things together with her kids, on the weekends we would go to the rainforest in Rio Grande; we found a waterfall and bathe in it all day how refreshing that was. Her dad was also there and Ana yes my future mother in law, she was very nice, but most of my time when they were around I would speak with Leon. He bought us *Lechon con Viandas*, Roast Pork with Vegetable, Yucca, Green Banana, and *pana*. He would have a beer, but I was strictly on water, or juice, I was Sober spiritually, my hopeless state of mind and body was arrested It was gone, But I would have to practice the principles everyday without hesitation, It was my medicine. I would pray and meditate all the time. I give thanks to God on a regular basis and I couldn't stop talking about it. Leon love to listen to me, because Leon was spiritual himself.

I and Teresita would go to our favorite spot at night The Caribe Hilton, we drink virgin Piña Coladas. Then after we walk to their private beach and share our thoughts. Teresita was the perfect woman for me because she like listening to my dreams and thoughts, sometimes the Imagination is all we have when things are not going our way. We can create a whole world in our own minds, and actually feel like we are there. Sometimes these thoughts come true, because up to today a lot of my thoughts have become a reality in some way.

As I continue to tell my story; allot of my dreams will come true. Though I was having a great time I really missed Jeanette. When I was with Teresita and her kids having fun, I would think of my daughter on the 14th floor, of that apartment in Bronx River. We spend a lot of time talking me and teresita about what we wanted to do and how we wanted our lives to be. We laughed a lot together and had much romance. I would start a conversation with her children and get to know them better. The trip was a success and the decision for me to stay with Teresita was the right one. My time in Puerto Rico would come to an end and it was time to go to NY to see my little girl. Teresita and the Kids traveled with me to meet my Family. I would make up my mind and make the decision that this will be my family. I asked Teresita, and she said yes.

We started making plans for our wedding and arrangements to move to Norfolk. We had a great time together and I finally had my family. Thank you God! We were all in the car the 3 kids Teresita and I. I yelled out "ok guys" where do you want to go? They didn't know what to say because we were in NY. So I said how about Rye play land, They all said "yeh" I felt like I just hit the lottery for 1 trillion dollars. There was no better feeling than that for me, I who just came out off the life I had. The car was full of glow and happiness; it's like we were on a magic carpet ride towards freedom. The way every family should feel; pure gratitude. Unfortunately I had to go back to work and everybody went back to their places. But I had a goal! I was getting married in September 1992 and my new wife and kids would be moving to Virginia in December 1992.

I was assigned to the USNS Mohawk again, but this time a different Captain and crew. Where was the Mohawk going to? Nowhere! It was staying stateside. I quickly made arrangements to rent an apartment in Norfolk Virginia, 7744 Enfield Avenue, Little Creek Road, North Shore Gardens, not too far from the base. The apartment would be available December 10th. The ship would go to the shipyard for 1 month in Boston. While I was there my future wife called me and asked me what I was doing? "I said" I was on watch; she said could you escape for a few days? I said go back to Puerto Rico? She said "no" I'm in Disney world with the kids and my parents; would you like to come over? I said I can't because I'm working and I'm paying off bills so when we get married I will be free of them. She says you don't need any money! I will buy your ticket and I have a rental car and I rented a small condo. I said hey! "I'm supposed to pay for that not you! She said ok, the next vacation you pay for it and I will pay this one. I asked the Captain, and he said if he can go to? I said "ahhh" he grinned and said, "knock yourself out go have fun" Captain Muir was one of the best Captains I ever sailed with as long as you did your job he was the coolest captain around. I flew from Boston to Orlando and for the first time I visited Disney World. I would talk with Leon a lot, 'in the old culture you had to spend time with the parents in order to have a good all around relationship. I'm still that way today.

When I arrived to Disney world Orlando Florida, I was amazed by the park. I was a child again and rushed to get on the rides. My new found future wife was bringing me into a world I never saw. It was a world of having fun with your hard earned money, not drugs and alcohol. I got own a ride and when it took off, the great movie ride, I felt so much happiness that I cried silently. I never thought one can have so much fun without alcohol, and drugs, it would be great therapy for me. The first thing that came to my mind was, I wanted to bring happiness to a lady, but this same lady was showing me how to live. I would only be motivated to continue on with my new life and sobriety.

Teresita was really a God given dream come true. I quickly forgot about any other woman I had in the past and she would become the front runner to be my all time queen. Sometimes people pray to God for miracles and wonder why they don't get them. God has a way of preparing you first for the miracle before getting it. So you must go to the school of God and pass. My time in Orlando would come to an end, for it was only a 4 day vacation. I would go back to the Mohawk and continue on with my plan.

Well the summer would come to an end and my wedding date was close to being a reality. I wanted to get married in Puerto Rico, so I told Teresita that I was going to rent a horse, and dress like an old Spanish soldier, then go to your job sweep you of your feet, and take you away. She was so excited about the dramatic scene I wanted to do. Unfortunately the plans would change and I couldn't leave Norfolk because our Tug was on 24 hour call, for the month of September. After thinking about it I said "phewwwww "that was going to take some bravery. I would do it! I'm that crazy!! I was in love with Teresita. I would do anything to excite her; I was on an emotional high and was dreaming like always. Plus I am very dramatic. I get it from my Mother.

The ship would have a call, in September. Guess what happened? We were told to go to Rosie Roads Puerto Rico. Tersita and I thought it would be a great idea to throw a little engagement party so the family can enjoy our new union. The Vargas family and Cruz family would once again be connected. Time to celebrate!! We put together a big party like a pre wedding party, at my aunts Celia's House in Cupey Puerto Rico. I invited the ships personal. My wife got some transportation for the ones that went, The First Officer, Navy Chief, engineer, and some others, but the captain had to stay. So here I am taking all these white boys who at one time in my life hated, to visit my family in Cupey P.R. That's to show you we could all change if we want to.

The party was a great success the sailors had a very good time and had 2nds and 3rds on the Lechon with Arroz con Gandules (roast pork and rice) and plenty of Ron Rico, and Bacardi, for them. I of course drank water, or soda. Before the night was over, I remember hearing, the First Officer, talking about how he was conceived in the Caribe Hilton, were his parents vacationed. I'm the type of guy that if you tell me something you want and I can give it to you, I will do it. So I took the sailors to the Caribe Hilton and they did not want to leave. Some went to the casino and some went to the club. The First Officer after enjoying several minutes said we have to get back. So I had to round everybody up and we go back to the ship. That night the First Officer did thank me for taking him there. I said don't thank me thank God.

The short wedding would take place in Norfolk. The attendees were my parents, her parents, my sister and her kids, Papito, Marisita, Marili, Jimmy, and Alexis, and her husband Jorge, Jeanette, and my brother Jose. Teresita didn't bring the boys. We were getting married at the courthouse in Norfolk. I would get 4 hotel rooms at the Airport Hilton in Norfolk. I paid for it all, than after the wedding I took everybody to old country buffet, It was too many to take to a regular restaurant. We then would drive to Maryland to my sister house and there my father cooked and my sister purchased a cake. We spend the night at the Sheraton Hotel in Maryland then continued to Atlantic City New Jersey where we stood at the Taj Mahall trump hotel.

When we got there, my wife had her corporate credit cards. I gave her cash and she got the room. They asked her for Identification and when she gave them her Puerto Rico Driver License they said "you come all the way from Puerto Rico"? That was my cue! I said yes we just got married and she has been dying to come to this hotel. We were giving a suite on a top floor overlooking the ocean and the casinos, for the price of 100.00, A 500.00 a night room. I'm not much of a gambler so I played slots until I lost 40 dollars, on the other hand my wife won 50.00 so we were ahead 10 bucks and went back to hotel suite and enjoyed it. We ordered dinner and had a candle light dinner and the view was great. I said to myself well! "Tyrone you are married and no looking at the woman any more". I would have to be responsible. I was ready for whatever showed up.

Our little vacation would end and I would go back to the ship and she would go back to Puerto Rico. I was starting not to like shipboard life to much anymore. It's like you are always saying goodbye to your family. I would feel lonely and worried that I still needed to get my little girl Jeanette. There would still be some more obstacles before Jeanette would officially live with me.

December arrived and my wife and kids would be there except Jeanette. I had to work out some things with her mom; however we spend Christmas in Norfolk. We started playing some salsa music and the lady next door knocked on our door and said "you can't play the music so loud' then called the cops on us. My wife had the look on her face like she was saying "where did this guy bring me to live." In Puerto Rico everybody is partying and hearing music for the Christmas holidays. My first reaction was to just get angry and call her racist, but we invited her over for some food and conversation and the next thing you know she is partying with us. She was lonely and needed some friendship. In sobriety I did learn to use my charm more than my anger. I wasn't perfect I would have my moments from time to time, however in the 12 steps we continue to take personal inventory of ourselves, so I kept an eye on myself only judging myself nobody else.

I started writing a daily inventory back in July of 1991 that would turn into a Journal. I would write about myself, family, politics, community, weird things that happen. Today I have over 7000 days of writing in these Journals and have written 14 books. My sponsor started teaching me about my heritage. The Taino Indians would be his teachings to me. I went to ceremonies, when travailing to Puerto Rico; I would go to Utuado and go to the Tainos Park in Caguana. I started to enlarge my spiritual life. I also learn about Native American life also. It was a big part of the knowledge I was gathering in my new life. A knowledge that will set me free from the bias education that was taught to me. I was starting to understand society.

In 1993 I would finally bring Jeanette to come live with me. It was pretty hard on my mother because she alone with Marisa raised her the first 8 years. I remember she was at the church with my mother waiting for me. I walked up to her and said are you ready to live with your dad? She said yes, but ran to my mother and gave her a big hug. We all cried because it was a strong moment in all our lives. She was very close to my mother and pretty much looked at her as she was her mom. We get in the car and Jeanette, and I, was freed. How that newspaper she played with was the key to our new life of happiness. People need to learn step 2 having an open mind.

I wanted to make more Money, so I requested to go to Piney Point Maryland, Merchant Marine School, for 8 weeks, so I could upgrade to Able Bodied Seaman which would pay 40,000 to 55,000 a year, with overtime. I would go every night to the library and study, along with some other guys who was in the class with me. The experience of studying and kind of going back to school was awesome. The diploma would mean more money so I was motivated by that alone. I pass the test and I was awarded the position. The first thing I did was start the process of getting a house.

I would go to my first ship as an AB—Able Bodied Seaman., I flew to Hurgada Egypt were I was a assigned to the USNS Lenthall. When I arrived in Hurgada it was so different. That was the ship I was on when I got beat up in Palma de Mallorca. I was in the Muslim world for the first time. They would pray several times a day and it was very hot. In the morning muster you would sweat just standing. By mid day you had to go inside because the heat was unbearable. My time there was brief, but I was able to do some good meditations and the local food was not that good. I remember bringing out candy for the kids who were poor and they would go crazy over it and the fresh water also. When you see kids in America not eating their food and throwing it away you get angry, because there are children starving to death in other countries. I think people should travel to poor towns so they could see how children would go crazy over a drink of cold water. People in America don't know how fortunate they are.

Whenever I walked into town, the people thought I was Egyptian. I am pretty much the same complexion as them, so I would talk with them and become friendly, as I was on an educational journey. We would leave and go to Jeddah Saudi Arabia; we were not given any liberty there. I really wanted to check out that country. We were going to some old interesting countries so I wanted the experience. We would leave the Red Sea and travel to the Mediterranean where I would get off the ship in Cartagena Spain, and fly back because I got hurt. I had to spend one night in Madrid, Spain so I stood in the Barrajas Hotel, then left the next day to NY than Norfolk. I would be home for Christmas.

I would end the year making, 39,000 and in June off 94 I moved into my first house. I paid 90,000 for it in Virginia Beach Timberlake section. I was so happy I felt good, taking care of my family and giving them the best, our Mortgage was 714.00 dollars a month. Between me and my wife who was also working at Montgomery Ward's, were making over 60.000, dollars a year. That was not bad for the 90s in the Hampton roads area of Virginia.

My first night I just sat in my living room for hours looking at the home and saying this is mine. Dreams do come true. I was in a good one!! Especially coming out of the nightmare I had. I owned a car, a home, had a great salary, a wife to die for, and 3 children. That to me was the human dream not the American dream, but a dream for any man in this world who loves his family and wants to provide for them. Although I was lost for many years; I always said I would become a real father and real husband. Throughout the time I was struggling with addiction, my daughter never needed any welfare or food stamps or Medicaid. I always provided for her, now I could even do better. I would never lose faith, as much as I wanted to die! I knew that this day would come. I would enjoy seeing my family live the way I saw families on TV like the Brady Bunch, or leave it to beaver, I can say that we were living the middle class life.

On to sea to make some money!! Rotan Honduras would be the next port, we towed over a barge for navy divers to work in that area. We spent 10 days there. It was a great experience the town was poor, but it was up and coming. A great tourist place for divers, the US navy had a lot to do with that. I would walk into town and meet people and ate in the restaurants one day I ate iguana meat; it was made in a stew and I liked it, over a bed of rice. I also went to their church one Sunday and was introduced by the pastor to the people. I have no idea why, but they were Grateful that the US was helping their economy so I guess they were just expressing their gratitude and I happened to be there so I accepted it. We would leave and the ship would go to the shipyard.

I was then assigned to the USNS Concord and I would make some serious money there, I kept growing spiritually and we were having a great time. I would have to leave my family for 6 months for the first time, and 1 month, before the deployment; my wife was already saying I don't want you to leave and would cry. I said "remember what I told you on the pier in Puerto Rico this is my Job". The problem with me was I had no High School Diploma so there was no way in hell I was going to make this type of money In Virginias Private sector. My credit was great and society trusted me again with loans. We were using my wife car that she shipped over from Puerto Rico it was pretty new, but small. I borrowed some money From Navy Federal Credit union and a bought a used van for 10.000 dollars. I had learned from my Father in law to keep your bills down and you would enjoy life better. Leon and Ana who had property in Florida would drive up from Florida and visit us. He loved the house especially the payment. I did not go over my head; between my car and House I was paying 1,000 a month that is not bad at all.

On my next deployment I was going to Europe, and I visited museums, castles and walk through their land like I was a student, learning about the old ways. I would go to restaurants, not bars full of woman looking for sailors. I talk to people in Spain and would learn a little about the culture. I was also learning about the Tianos so there was a little bitterness there. I felt different about Spain. I remember having a conversation with a man over the scars that Spain left in Puerto Rico and other Indian countries. He said yes your right, Spain really left an ugly scar in Puerto Rico, but he said that was the way things were. The inquisition was brutal and savage, but today a person could be whoever he wants to be in your country, whereas in some countries people are still slaves. I thought about that and there was a lot of truth in that, however we are far away from freedom, in order to be free you must live amongst freedom from oppression and even though you could make a great life, silently, others are still trying to make life hard on you. People throwing in my face go back to your country is not what I call freedom. I was living great and was grateful, but I'm not a dog you can't throw a bone at, then become your best friend, materialism is not freedom" to be accepted unconditionally is"

I remember one night while sitting in the living room of my new home; I started thinking about when I was in Grammar school. how I use to draw pictures. These pictures were of a boat and a house with a car and family as I shared a few chapters ago. The boat came from the show McHale's Navy a program I grew up watching. The house came from the summer trips to upstate New York where we use to go. The law of attraction is very true! If you are always visualizing something you want, you will get it. When I look back at my life, I say to myself, why I allowed so many obstacles to get in my way. God doesn't put obstacles in front of us we do. We just like to blame everything on God. "Oh It's his will' no it isn't, it's our screw up that causes us to live so rotten. I do believe that we have a destiny, no matter what we do our destiny will happen. In my case I'm a writer, I have found my bad decisions something that I can share with people, but suppose I went through life the correct way, Finished High School, went to college, never was in gangs, or a user of drugs? I would still be a writer. I would be writing someone else's bad life. God does not destroy your life so than you could prove you love him. That is pure Bullshit. We the people love to blame God for all our short comings; so we can have a justifiable reason to struggle.

When I became an Able Bodied Seaman, my attitude changed. I was no longer feeling low self esteem. I always ask questions if I didn't know something. I had outgrown that fear. I was steering the ship in and out of port, I steered thru the Suez Canal and steered while having ships alongside. My next step would be to become an Officer that's right 3rd Mate would be my next goal. That would put me at 80,000 a year and on route to becoming a Captain. MSC had a lot of Captains that started just like me from the bottom and a lot of Abs was becoming 3rd Mates, so it wasn't hard to do, you had to study, on the job training or go to School.

In March of 1994 the ship ported in Cyprus a country shared by Greece and Turkey, I went to a church and learned of an alcohol support group there. I participated and met a Friar or Priest who was from the States living there Fr. O' Brien, he was from New Jersey, we talked spiritually and I learned much from him. The next day I rented a Hotel Room to get away from the ship; my room had a balcony facing the mountains. It was a great view. I thought it would be a great spot for meditation, so I burned some incense and smudged myself and while looking at the mountains. I start to pray and ask God to guide me in my new life. I then closed my eyes and just started seeing visions of mountains, waves, and people. I opened my eyes and saw something! It looked like it was some sort of energy moving. The experience was awesome; however I got nervous and went into the room, for my mind showed some negativity. I then said to myself, "why did I do that"? I actually connected to something and I should have listened within. "I blew it" but I did noticed one thing, I wasn't wasting my time in this new form of spirituality, there was a connection made! It was pure energy, and it's good. My fear was of ignorance not of the energy I saw, because while I had my eyes closed I felt as I was in another world, I felt real peace, sensation, something that only a supreme being can give you, God was watching, and he/she or both, is pure love.

I would go that night to the church and talk to the friar and he said enjoy it and continue on your path. The ship left and we stopped at a couple more ports and on April 24th we went to Haifa Israel. There was a trip to Jerusalem available for the crew, so I went to Jerusalem. It was a blessing to experience Jerusalem, there I went to the Wailing Wall, and prayed. I also went inside and prayed while Jews were praying. I became part of Gods people no segregation for me, for I am a student of God and I shall learn all beliefs if I have to; that is just the way I am. To be closed minded is why we live in such a rotten world were war is the God everyone accepts, to destroy someone, because his or her culture or beliefs are different.

When the tour was over we were giving some time to shop. I decided to find a nice place to sit and within my mind and heart, I talked to Jesus. I was in the Garden of Gethsemane where Jesus had the last supper. My question was? I know your message had nothing to do with the Massacre of thousands of Indians in the Americas where they used your name, all native South and Central and North American. Though I don't go to Church regularly or call myself a Christian, I believe in you, I just don't believe in the ones passing the Message. Why do people kill or enslave people in the name of God? Nothing happen, I continued" Jesus" you are one of the greatest messengers of God! and what so funny is; that if you would to come back, the same people who preach about you would treat you the same way they did 2000 years ago and betray you. How confused are the people, but, some of us do know the message, and the message I get when I read your parables are to love unconditionally and not judge. I just wanted to say that to you. As I walked away I felt as if I was surrounded by love.

When I read the book The Indian Chronicles, By Jose Barriero, the inquisition of the Tainos was brutal. I believe the church owes Jesus and God an apology for using his name in vain. I guess the ones that pushed it 500 years ago have paid the price already. Some people in Puerto Rico say the Tianos were all eliminated. There are no more Tainos, well there are very much a lot of them saying they are still here, and practicing their ancestor's way of life. I know, I feel like I am one of them. Not full, but part of the race. You can never destroy a culture that works within; you could only destroy the community.

Our next port of visit would be Rhodes Greece. The place looked like a kingdom, there was a large wall surrounding the town, when you walked through the gates it was an old city, but well kept, museums with paintings, sculptures, and lots of small cafes. I was really blessed that I was able to get sober and revisit these countries. I now looked at these countries with sobered eyes and was able to learn history on its natural turf. I meditated by the water and saw many visions of people and good things to come. I started buying more books that taught me how to work with the inner self. I was going to learn about the subconscious mind, something that if practiced correctly could lead to a better life.

I believe that we continue traveling we never die, our spirits keep coming back in order to accomplish things we didn't in our last life, every life is a learning experience and should be lived to the fullest. The subconscious mind has all the information of your past and present life. I may sound kind of weird, but it's better to practice that than practice hate, and worry, about the future like most people.

Spiritual leaders, get assassinated because they are in someone's way maybe "evil" what the assassins fail to understand is, while one leader dies another is born and continues where the other left. I didn't know Dr. Pedro Albizu Campos; but here I am talking about him in 2012, trying to share with Puerto Ricans, that only herd negative news about him.

Have you ever bumped into someone that says hi to you like they know you, but you say, who's that? Or a baby who just smiles at you while walking on the street in a weird way, not everything has an explanation, sometimes we should leave it alone and believe, like the friar in Cypress told me just enjoy it.

There was a day, we were in port, and one of the guys invited me to hang out with them and go to a club; where there would be allot of woman or street woman. I said no I have a family and that is not how a live today. he says Tyrone when you are out here we have to do whatever it takes to get laid, plus you don't know what your wife is doing while you are gone, I was centered and in control of my emotions, I laughed and said no. I thought about what he said, but there was a man there who listened and he tells me, we are responsible for us it does not matter what our partners do it's what we do, there are no bonus points in life for justified adultery, because you feel your wife might have falling to it. I had to take that advice, because it made sense. Now if the love is gone then that is a different story you divorce and move on.

We are so enslaved to our character defects and live this life of false hope and think we are on the right path, because we go to church and drop 10% in the basket, but there is more to life than that. Jesus was spiritual not religious he meditated and prayed outdoors and never collected a dime from no one. He was assassinated, because he pissed of the self righteous. How many will kill him today?, if he came in the form of a black man, or Latino man, white man, whatever., they would call him crazy and leave him up for ridicule, But didn't he come in the form of a regular Joe last time. Maybe Jesus did come back and left, because no one believed him. In meditation you learn, because in meditation you listen to God, in prayer you talk to God. This is just my opinion.

While in these countries, I would pick up rocks that I felt were special and bring them home and put them in a bowl. What I love about spirituality is you are on a journey of finding who are, and why you are here, you don't beat yourself up when you make a character error you try to change it and move on. I would have a lot to learn and was always asking my sponsor questions and reading. I purchased a lesson from a teacher called Paramahansa Yogananda from the self realization fellowship, and it taught me how to meditate better. It had 50 lessons and I did each one to the best of my ability. The benefit of all this was reading. I was educating myself with life and getting better with my reading and writing skills.

I was growing quick, I remember when going to some of the alcoholic support groups, I would get bored to death listening to people with more sober time than me, sound as they just came out of a rehab. My friendship circle was very small, because when you become spiritual people tend to believe you are boring. There was one character defect that was always my hardest.

Being faithful to one woman is not that easy, no matter how much you love; there is always temptation and do woman love to temp us on a daily basis. I believe some of us men need to go to faithful rehab. In the beginning of my new marriage, my wife and I would have that little argument, about me looking at other woman while at the mall or the beach. When I was staying in Puerto Rico with my wife and the thought of me living there instead of moving to Norfolk was a choice, I said, I won't last 1 month here. The woman in Puerto Rico to me is the prettiest woman on the planet and some could be very aggressive even if you are waking with your wife. I was used to meeting woman on a weekly basis so just being with one was going to be pretty hard, but just like that as God is my witness I have been faithful to my wife since day one and that makes it 20 years, the woman in Puerto Rico always dress very nice, not like here where jeans are the number one clothes for ladies. I love a lady that dresses like one, not dress like a man with pants all the time.

I was very honest when I got sober, and told my wife I prefer to live in Norfolk, at this time. I need to be stronger before moving to Puerto Rico.

There is lust and there is love we love our wives, but lust for other woman and that is a character defect we all need to change including woman. Guilt is something recovering addicts can't have so we have to stay faithful, because if not it may cause a relapse in our recovery. To drink is to die, to stay sober is to live. {Big Book Alcoholics Anonymous} That was my mind set and believe me I had plenty opportunities. In my opinion a married man has no business going to clubs with his friends, and the same goes for woman. You need to check yourself here, you are married with children, a good life while spoil it by surrounding yourself with temptation. You could always go to a restaurant with a friend if you need a drink and conversation. For me if I need to get away from my family it's because maybe I am not happy with them. Being honest with oneself is something that just makes me stronger. I'm not saying that being around a lot of pretty woman makes me weak, but really! Why go to a club with your friends when you can't get involved with the opposite sex? I understand I sound like weak link but he is a scenario.

Say you are at the club with your friends not with your wife. You had a few drinks and this hot mama comes and ask you to dance, your friends cheer you on and you dance with her, she's better looking than your wife, she likes you and invites you to her table, you say no I'm married, and beat yourself up for not going, then you go home. She is on your mind and not your wife. You're feeling reborn because some chick tried to pick you up. You are now fighting the thoughts that are coming to you and it creates an uncomfortable feeling and your wife starts to notice it. This may not happen to everybody, but I guarantee you It will bother you a little.

Let me tell you of a dream I had at sea. In my dream I was having an affair with a beautiful woman, sexy, everything she was great the perfect 10. I was going to leave my wife for her. Leon my father in law was pleading with me that I shouldn't do it. That I was destroying all the good relations I had built with them. I said I am sorry Leo I have to have this woman. I went to the wedding and married the lovely Girl, but after I said I do, the form of her pretty face turned into a pig and then a sinister evil person. I jumped out of that dream shaking with fear and I learned that everything is not what it seems to be sometimes. The dream was telling me something.

The ship headed back to Norfolk and I would put another successful deployment behind me. I would learn new things and teach my wife and kids. They learned if they wanted to. We didn't go to church because, I did not see the point the kids never listened and it was the same stuff over and over, fear of going to hell. I like others, believe that religious people are working on staying out of hell, spiritual people have been through hell and are trying to stay out. I believe, we make our own Heaven and Earth right here on Earth, it is how we live it's what carries us through life, we are what we think, and our thoughts create our world. I have proven this already in my story.

Like always when I got home we traveled to either my sister house in Maryland or NY to see my parents and eat some good Puerto Rican food. In the early 90s there was nothing in Hampton Roads Puerto Rican, some stores may carry adobo seasoning, or something, but no restaurants. We would also go to Manhattan and my wife would buy clothes, and we all shop. In 1994 we started thinking of opening a business, but that would come later on, however it was floating in our minds. My wife was starting to get tiered of me leaving all the time to sea. My dream of becoming a Captain would have to be dropped, but I would take it one day at a time and only hope to make the right decision. Our children were growing and enjoying life. We would teach them and would have prayer circles where the children would talk and meditate as a family. We had no friends just ourselves, but that is all we needed

The spirituality I talk about is my own opinion. I have learned so much of so many religions and cultures that I just merged it together. I found sobriety and it worked for me, in no way am I saying that whatever you practice is wrong. I respect all religions, because they all have something to do with faith in a higher power. Whatever it takes for change is what is required to practice. I went from a lost soul to a powerful force of wisdom, vision, and spiritual strength. To be honest! I think the best explanation on how to live comes from the movie Star Wars; "Don't give into the dark side of the force". It's that simple. We all have within, good and evil, it depends on you which will you choose. I drank and drugged for almost 18 years of my life because, I gave into hate, envy, despair, lust, and the list could go on, but when I gave into the good side, I found sobriety, happiness, love, respect, and abundance, that list could go on also. We could sit around all day and talk about devils and bad entities, but all of our life comes down to us. We all have the gift of free will. God does not brush your teeth or put on your clothes neither does the devil, it's up to me every day, what I decide to do. Like I said this is what I have learned and will continue to grow using these methods.

The sad part of my growth was how my mother did not give me her blessings, because she felt that if I wasn't going to church that It didn't matter, I was not saved. We would argue a lot about my new found spirituality and she would blame my sponsor for introducing me into the Taino culture which is Puerto Rican. I don't understand why people have to always become car salesman with religion, "no this one is better". If their religion is so great, why are they miserable? I would go to church, but would feel like a phony, because, I didn't want to be there, eventually I would not go at all. I found something in the 12 steps! My new spiritual journey has kept me sober. I was in control of my decisions again, not alcohol and drugs. I was faithful to my wife, I did my Job, was honest, was responsible, great father, helpful toward others how can evil be part of that. I was learning about myself and trying to change the old me and produce a new me. I can speak to anyone about God. I even spent time in the holy land Israel, and followed and acknowledged the Christian walk; I just don't agree that Christians are the only righteous spiritual people on earth. I'm sorry if I hurt anyone, but we are all part of the spiritual circle of God.

I was very hurt that my mother was not happy with my new life. Her son was becoming a successful human. This is what kills me about Religion they practice segregation more than the racial people of the 60s. Sometimes I feel like starting a church called the human race for we are all the same and whatever you believe in its accepted as long as it brings positive results toward love and happiness for mankind. John Lennon "Imagine" what a beautiful song I wonder if some people understood what it meant. "Why must good people die young" I don't know! It's like evil gets angry every time someone comes out and starts moving the people. Evil than finds someone to kill them, I guess we will continue to try.

My father in law who was a strong Catholic never acted that way. I remember when I was overseas I would collect rocks. I use to bring them back from all over the world. He one day created a symbol using the rocks, buy placing them on a large rug, and it would take up a good section of my living room. We would sit there as a family and pray, do ceremonies, and meditation. Religion has its good points and it has its bad points. It could be the same as racism segregation of people something I believe God does not like much. Hurricanes and destruction toward human life could sometimes be positive, why? Because when all is gone and we are without the things we need. We become humble, and if your enemy showed up with a row boat in a flood the average person would jump and thank him. Why is it, when we have our backs against the wall is when we become humble? If we could act the same all the time as when we were in dire need of help, what a great world this would be.

1995 would be a good year! I would learn much more about myself, along with questions I had about my life. I also read the book The Indian Chronicles By Jose Barriero, The books is a Journal written by "Deguilo Colon" his Christian name, his real name was Guikan a Taino who become the interpreter for The admiral Christopher Columbus. The journal was written in Castilian and found in a convent in Santo Domingo, according to the book. It talked about the brutal Spanish Inquisition and how the Spaniards were cruel towards the Indians. The "Phoenix Rising" By Mary Summer Rain. That book explains about the Earth Changes and how many terrible things will happen. I would learn allot from those books, and learn to appreciate life for every day I wake up breathing, because they is one thing we all know that's guarantee, and that is death, but like I said in another Chapter only the temple of the spirit dies, the spirit lives forever. Another book I read was "Black Elk Speaks" the story about an Oglala Sioux written by John G Neihardt. I also read several others that had to do with inner workings and understanding society's real motive. I did go through a lot of emotions, because when you are changing you tend to want to preach to everyone. When you find something good you want to share it with everyone, and some of us don't know how to. I made more enemies than friends on the ship, some thought I was crazy, I would get confused.

One night I had a dream with a spiritual man who I was reading about at the time and who was deceased. He was standing on a diving board looking down into a pool with no water, as he is looking down he said! "I will take 30 days to think about this" than he turns toward me and says, "you tell them not to smoke and they smoke". That was a powerful message when you think about it, how many people you tell them not to do something, but out of curiosity they do it. I learned to preach through my actions. My actions would get more attention than my words. I recall a man who was on a ship with me when I was an active drinker and he saw the new me, and he asked me "what in hell did you do" you look so different and the way you carry yourself in port it's amazing. So there you go actions speak louder than words.

In the spring of 1995, they needed some mariners, to work aboard a ship for 2 months. I took the Job and off I was to Rome then Venice Italy were the ship was in a shipyard. I would visit the famous Piazza San Marko, eat at restaurants and ride in water taxis everywhere, although it was nice, you really need to be with your wife, because by yourself it's a waste. I will one day take my wife there. The crazy thing was the Square was always flooded with water when it rained. We stood at a hotel in town. I was enjoying Europe in a different way I admired all the art and the old country sites. The Churches were old and the buildings were to, the food was awesome and the bakeries were the best, it was like going back into time. I thought of living in Europe, if I were single I probably would off. We were there for 2 months, I went to several museums and looked at art work, went to shows, and ate at the best restaurants in town. I was getting extra money to eat, for the mess hall was closed for repairs and they gave us enough per Diem, for me to give myself the life of a king. I walk all over the place just sightseeing and experiencing an old European city people only dream of seeing. God has done for me what I couldn't do for myself. I wish I could off have had my whole family on the ship when deployed.

After the repairs were done we were off to Naples Italy for 30 more days. While in Naples I did the same. Naples is more Like Old New York city. I flew back to the United States so I could prepare for our family trip to Disney world.

We drove to Florida to spend a week there, we had a great time. My children had smiles all the time they were there, I did also. When we arrived to Disney World we took a family picture and we enjoyed every minute. I was so happy to see them laugh and I would play along with

Jeanette, Leonell, and Andre. Leon was also there and he also got on the rides with us. Leon loved being with us because he knew we were a new family full of love and happiness. We were humble; we did not over spend and were happy with anything we got. We didn't spend that much so we were able to go to Puerto Rico that Christmas.

Leon and Pipo my brother in law paid for a condo in luqullo beach and gave it to us as a Christmas present. It was right on the beach and the Rainforest was close to it. We went to the *Yunque* and found a waterfall and bathe all day. It felt like paradise and the feeling of being in old times was what we sensed we were living. The next day we went to *Caguana* the Taino Park and this time met a practicing Taino Indian called *Baracutey*. He invited us to his house and we had a great time. He showed us a lot of Taino ways and we spend the night in his home. He had a big 2 story cement house and it was surrounded by trees and vegetation, "I'm going to tell you" only an Idiot could starve in Puerto Rico. Puerto Rico is so rich in food, I understand why Dr. Pedro Albizu Campos wanted Nationalism instead of being part of the United States, There are resources are all over.

The next day we left, but we found a new friend in Puerto Rico. Me myself I was proud to say that I am Tiano, Puertorriqueño. I was walking on the grounds of my ancestors. On Christmas Day I wore Indian boots, which is more Native American. I also wore an Indian Choker around my neck and my wife wore a beautiful Indian Dress, we walked around San Juan and got some attention, we even went to the Caribe Hilton for lunch, I did not care I was just showing Puerto Ricans that the Indian part of our heritage has not been forgotten and was still very much alive. Yes I am a radical; I'm not a phony! I will represent all that is part of me and be proud.

Latin countries acknowledge their indigenous people whereas in Puerto Rico they try to say the Tainos were wiped off the planet. I can't stand that about my country. I love talking Spanish, because, It's part of our diversity, but I am also part Taino, and you would only hope Puerto Rico Tourism would be more involved. Every time I go to that park it's empty. They only want to show the Spanish part, what they don't understand is tourist want to see everything, you think the Mayan temple is not visited by tons of tourist every year In 2011 they even made a movie about the Mayan Calendar. Puerto Rico has so many artifacts to share, but all we do is kiss ass and try to show that we are just like America. I was starting to see how Puerto Rico was trying to be so much like the United States. You can see the ghettos and drugs becoming a cancer that would hurt our island. Puerto Rico would be almost a lost economy, People getting killed over a hit of heroin.

We would Fly back home and get ready to start 1996. When I shared with my sponsor about *Baracutey* he sound a little angry, you see he wanted me to find this other Taino tribe who was in Ponce, but I found *Barucutey* instead! And my feelings when I met him were good not fearful. In spirituality we feel we don't look and we follow the spirit not the person who advises us, people could be wrong, that is why we must always meditate on everything we do. I at the time didn't know, but my relationship with my sponsor was getting sour quick. My wife didn't like how he was acting neither. I guess I was growing and God had another path for me. My sponsor was just suppose to guide me not control me. The good thing was, my wife and I always had dialogue, and we always in the morning drank coffee and discussed our life situations.

That year we would be introduced in to the sweat lodge. It's a dome type of tent, with a pit and to place rocks that were sitting in fire. The hot rocks would be placed into the pit, than blessed water, and it would create a steam bath. The idea was to go back into the womb of the mother and come back out reborn, to leave your problems and bad character there; spirits would also come into the lodge. I remember in one experience, I could not stop from painting my face with dirt from the ground I was sitting on, it must have been a child because, I just wouldn't stop painting my face. I would circle my eyes with my fingers full of dirt and rub them and down my face cheeks, I would spread the earth on my face. The leader would tell us control the spirit because they could dominate you. I continued to play with the spirit. In that same lodge I heard for the first time the name Dr. Pedro Albizu Campos. A woman who was Puerto Rican was the one saying it. And she said to avenge his goals. Me myself the woman was making it up, because it was her voice. However I wanted to find out who he was, so I asked my wife and she told me he was a communist of the past. I worked for the Government and that word would put me right at a halt, but it would always stay in my head. I felt that my wife neither new to much about him because whenever someone is not liked by Governments they are called Communist. People are suckers for that word.

I left it alone, but, I also remembered how they gave Malcolm X, a bad name. I did the research, and I learned he wasn't. This happen in Greenwood Lake NY, I was not liking to much these ceremonies and my children and wife were starting to get a little scared so I stopped going. I believe what they were doing is mixing Native American with Santeria. I did not want to mess with that because people sometime use that to hurt people. I remember an old girlfriend of mind that practiced sanitaria; she once told me she put the names of people in the freezer when she had problems with them. I said if we ever have a problem put me next to the roast Beef just in case I get hungry.

I continue learning Native American culture and was just trying to change and grow into a higher consciousness with my creator. In that same year something big spiritually will happen and give me conformation that I was on the right path. On my next deployment the ship again went to Israel and I took the trip to Bethlehem, but it was in a zoo in Haifa that I would go to where I noticed it. There was a large Birdcage with Eagle, Eagle Owl, Vultures, and on the floor there was a feather inside out of reach. I picked up several, but I wanted that one also. I could not reach it, this large Eagle which was black or very dark walked towards the fence, In Native American crafts we make spiritual things with these feathers. We could use it for smudging, or part of a spiritual tool. I looked at the large bird and asked if you give me that feather, I will always honor it! Nothing happen! I say to myself, "am I losing my dam mind! In Israel asking a bird for a feather" as I walked away in disbelief! The bird grabbed the feather, and put it through the hole of the fence like he was passing it to me. I dropped to my knees and said we are all connected and I am on the right path. There could be a thousand explanations!, but that is what I will believe and still today I have that feather and I honor it.

My marriage life was starting to take a turn for the worse my Daughter was not cooperating much with my wife and I was gone half the year and sometimes would do a turnaround so she was left with all the house responsibilities and it was starting to get to her. Teresita is a Puerto Rican from a well known family in Rio Pierdras. When she would appear at the Bakeries they knew her, when she went to the bank the Manager would say how your Dad is, she would go to Plaza las Americas with over 1,000 bucks in her purse, and she was a the lead singer in her brother part time band *conjunto zinigual.* Hampton Roads in the 90s was not the best place for Puerto Rican woman like that, the natives were pretty nasty with Spanish speaking people and her job paid her peanuts next to what she was used to having. Teresita is very smart and studied at the University Of Puerto Rico, but when she got pregnant and had her first child had problems, she dedicated herself to her child, which worked out because he was able to get better. She became Vice President of Vargas Hardware, a plumbing Supply company started by her Dad in the 50s; she also had her Real Estate license. She spoke perfect English and has a great personality and real pretty, you would think she be married to a Doctor not me. That was one of the things that worried me about her, could she live without that life, so I told her if she wanted to live in Puerto Rico and we could start this all over again? Her answer was this; I just want you to be here with me. I don't care where I live, in Puerto Rico the guys were after my money not my love and you have proven to me by bringing me here and buying a house and loving and caring for my kids. I started asking the spirit for help, for a new transition to another job where I would not have to leave my family anymore and like the Jeannie in the bottle your wish is my command for the Universe listens to your thoughts. 1996 would be over in comes 1997.

Chapter 8

The year the turbulence would start. I started praying about my Future and ask God to help me with it. I knew I would lose my family if I didn't, and I certainly did not want that happen. I told my wife let me grab a couple more ships pay off some bills and in 1998 I would quit. I reported to Bayonne New Jersey to get my new assignment and guess what ship? I was going on, the USNS Sirius, The First ship I started this Merchant Marine Journey on. I felt as it was my last, because, life is a circle, once you go around its time to move on. I would fly to UAE United Arab Emirates, I fly to England and there I bought a newspaper and started reading it, I noticed that English in England was a little different and I talk to some of the people there. I am as social as they come! I could start a conversation in the middle of a war. They talk the same as I've heard them on Television and it was exciting to actually experience it. I didn't get an opportunity to into town for it was there only on a connecting flight stop. I then would fly to United Arab Emirates. All together something like 14 hours of flying time. UAE is a really nice place almost like NYC a lot of money and the famous Gold district where I bought my wife some jewelry. The Muslim world is like any other they work, they have families, and they pray, a little more than most people. They demand respect, and you can't go over there acting like a fool. They have some very strict laws over there. They do like the good life and they play it to the tee, Cigars and all. They are also great salesman they will not let you go until you buy something. When you walk into their store with something from another store, they tell you," let me see" this is no good "mine is very good' 100%. Trust me". If you don't buy it you won't have a minute peace. Those would be the 2 ports we would go to in Dubai, UAE, until we would leave the Red sea and Persian Gulf areas. Overall it was a nice experience, but since we were restricted from travelling around the country I kept is pretty simple.

We started our journey back home to Norfolk. I was working on the bridge on this trip, which means I was driving; it took several days as we sailed through the red sea down than back up the Persian Gulf and into the Med. We made several stops in Italy, Spain, than Rota and strait to Norfolk, "How funny life is" I would go on that ship in December off 1988 as a dishwasher now I'm driving the ship back to Norfolk. It's just to show what a person could accomplish when the word I can't is taken out of their vocabulary. Although my hope of being a Captain was looking like a dream not to come true, I prayed a lot, because I felt this was it as a sailor! I wanted so much to be a captain, but it was between my family and my career, I said if my wife could give up all she had to be with me, I could do the same. The only question I had to myself? Is where I'm going to make 50,000 a year with no High School diploma in Virginia? We got back to Norfolk and I told my wife I would start looking for work, but I'm not quitting until I find a good Job, she agreed, I know she loved me, but being broke could bring a lot of problems she would prove me wrong one day.

A couple of weeks after we got home, I broke my ankle on the ship, I was in cast and home on compensation. 2 months of Tyrone in the house. I would go to the supermarket and grab one of those handicapped electric cars and drive around like a kid, I almost destroyed the place. Yahooooo I was having some fun. I would go buy something at the supermarket just to drive those things. I was so energetic that not even my leg in a cast could stop my motivation to have fun. Two months would pass and I would go back on another ship the Concord getting underway August 22, 1997. I still felt that the Sirius was my last voyage, but I went with the flow. I was awarded the Job of Ships Fire Marshall which means you could write your own Overtime. I was going to make a financial killing on this voyage. I told my wife that we would be able to save some money. She accepted it so I start my preparation for the trip.

That Tuesday Night, I would have a dream that I and my wife were In Bronx River where I grew up, and we were running away from 3 tornados coming at us. We ran to a building and hid from the tornado and I said what do we do now? Then I woke up. Awhile back I had broke my friendship with my sponsor, because me and my wife felt as he was not the same person I met. We did not hate him, I still today love the guy for bringing me the message, but he was getting to pushy so we broke up our friendship.

On Thursday the 21, of August, I would hear that my son got accused of something he didn't do. I got home early, because the ship was sailing the next day at 9am. I got very sacred so I went to see a lawyer; my wife was working, so I didn't tell her so she wouldn't get upset. I went to a lawyer not far from home and when we got there I broke down into a crying frenzy. I saw bad times ahead and was worried of how my wife was going to react. I knew the charges were not true so I would get ready. I kept all the kids with me and said let's just pray and stay cool. I went to pick up my wife at work and told her. She went berserk! Our family was being torn apart by an outsider. At that time I wanted to just shoot the people who were accusing my son, they knew they were wrong and my anger had returned. I was getting that Southern Hospitality. I would channel my anger in order to do the right thing. I knew God would get involved when I needed him. The next day early we all went to the ship. I left my family on the pier in the car and told them, I would be back; my wife was almost losing her mind, when I looked at her I knew I had to stay. I asked to speak with the Captain. The Chief Mate instead came to see me. I told him what had happen and asked permission to be excused from the ship. He said that the excuse wasn't just that I would have to take the trip and wait till I'm Relieved by someone. I said "Ok "I thanked him for everything MSC had done for me, out of my back pocket came a letter of resignation. That I had written the night before. The mate say's "You crazy "you going to quit your job, what about your career, and security? I told him in these words "what is a career and money when your loved ones are being torn apart, my love for them is more important than any career and Money." I left the bridge and walked down the gangway, and as I walked "I said God I just walked away from my security please help me" When I got into the car I said "I quit my Job we are going to deal with this as a family". When we got home the cops were waiting for my son. Right in front of us and the neighbors he was handcuffed and taken away. My wife cried out loud my 2 little kids started to cry and I felt as my whole life had dropped. I followed the cop car to the station he would have to spend the weekend in Jail till Monday. We bailed him out.

My farther in law sent me a Check for 3,000 dollars to get the lawyer started and told me he was on his way. That I wasn't alone and he told me what I did was noble that God would not leave you alone. I had 15,000 saved in a 401 k I had just started several years ago and took all of it out after penalties I had 10,000 left exactly what the lawyer ask for, he knew the case would never get to court. I did also. I reassured my wife all will be good. My son was set on 2,000 Bail which was a $ 200 bond not that much of a case, but it would cost me my career which was worth a lot more than that. We would pray every day for the accusers and my son that all would work out.

I got a job making 5 dollars an hour, but I went to the adult learning center and took my GED and failed it, but had an idea of what I needed to study. I switched jobs and became a security guard, after I saw people stealing in the store constantly I quit and got another job. I would take my GED again and pray to God every time I did not understand the question. A month later I was on my way to Join ECPI I was thinking of getting a new career, but while driving there I looked to the right and decided to drive to Colonial Chevrolet. I put in for a Salesman Job and lied that I had a High School diploma hoping I passed the last test I took. I was hired and took 1 week of classes at the dealership. They told me I would start on Monday, but I needed to bring in my High school Diploma. I started getting butterflies in my stomach. I felt it was a good job, and though it was commission, I could do it. However I had no High School diploma. When I got home, I checked the mail. I got the letter with the results, I told my wife I'm too scared to open it, she said "open it Tyrone" I did, I passed! Yelling in happiness, I jumped like a child who just got a big toy. I told my wife that I was going to attack that job with a passion. That there is a power of the universe and that power was God.

I was told that I would have to say something in the sales meeting by the trainer so I thought out something. I remember the Eco newspaper had an article on how Hispanics were growing in Hampton roads, that there was over 50,000 Hispanics in the area. When Fridays, sales meeting came I was called up, here I am looking at all these southern Salesman and my Nuyorican ass going to make a speech. I said my name, and told them were I'm from and said; "how can all you salesman bypass the 50,000 Hispanics in the area at the same time showing the article", "well I guess I will take over that department and show you all" the GM, Mr. Blais loved my attitude, and he started advertising *sé habla español* in all the advertisement in the Virginian Pilot. Yes! I started that around here, Tyrone Garcia. I am a headliner baby. The Virginian Pilot also put out an article about how area businesses were noticing the Hispanic growth, I have both articles saved.

I started working at Colonial Chevrolet in December of 1997. I would sell 10 cars in my first month of January 98 and made 3000.00 a month, on average. I was wearing a suit like a professional and I liked the job, though I didn't get any Hispanics, I sold cars to plenty white folks and Black folks. I even sold trucks to Red necks. I was looking at the money, not the color, I was focused. For a Latino you think I would be hated! Well at Colonial everybody liked me the customers also. I had this energy in me that people will feel it as I walked by with passion and confidence to do my job. I would always add humor to everything just like a Puerto Rican.

In February I would get my biggest challenge John H. It was a small deal, but I wanted to win every negotiation I got into, it would take me 2 days of negotiating to close that deal. I only got paid 100.00, but it was the principle he told me "he wasn't buying" and I told him he was. I finally sold him a brand new 98 Lumina. When he would come to get his oil changes we would talk, we had become friends something I did with all my customers, because networking and pyramid building is the Key to successful sales.

I sold a car to a man two days later. When I called him to ask how was his vehicle his wife asked me what other cars I had? which meant she wanted to buy a car. She came in a bought a car also. I did 12 the next month and average about 10-11 a month not a lot, but there was a lot of salesman there and what I was looking for was consistency. I also blew a lot of sales because I was new and mad plenty mistakes. I was in the use car department, but could also sell new ones, however the money was in used cars, In my first year I made over 38.000 and bought my wife a Brand new Monte Carlo for Christmas of 98. I put a big Christmas ribbon and bow on the hood and brought it to her job she was very happy. I of course took the old Van.

In September of 98 the lawyer called me and said that the case was dismissed, my son's record would stay clean, and I was making close to what I was making in MSC plus had 401k plus health benefits. I was starting a new career wearing a suit and sold over 100 cars in my first year, not bad.

1999 would come in with a bang at 10 am on January 1, 1999 I sold the first car of the year and made 300.00 dollars in commissions. I sold 12 cars in Jan. and would sell 13 in February.

In 1998 Puerto Rican restaurants started to pop up. The San Juan restaurant and El Latino deli and Bakery, were your first ones. I went to both and was proud someone broke the ice; the lines were outside at the San Juan it was on Independence Blvd. The food was ok, but people were complaining about the price something that was a big problem in the area, people wanted to eat good and cheap, but at the time the ingredients for Puerto Rican food was expensive. Goya products were high.

My son was doing very good he got a job and met Jackie who would become his wife later on. We were doing fine and we were growing again our Mortgage payment was on time, but we also had to get rid of all the credit cards we had, Although I made decent money the 97 year had killed us and we were so behind we could never get ahead, It was a rough situation for us but thank God the Car business was doing good for us. Things were starting to get better very quick. But they would be more obstacles ahead.

In February of 1999, my wife sent our son Andre to El Latino Deli and Bakery to buy pastries he came back saying they were closed. I went over to find out what happen and there was a letter on the door saying that they were selling the business because of some problems. I would go there a lot and the place had a customer base already. We had talked about having a business before and felt this was a calling. I called the Number that was left on the door and asked them what was there price?. They gave me the price of 55,000 dollars at the time. I didn't know anything about owning Business. They wanted 20,000 down, and payments. I ask to take a look and to me the price was alright because it was a turnkey operation, construction alone you are looking at more plus paying rent while you have no money coming in. I told them ok. I'll get back to you, here I am with −20 in my bank account trying to buy a business, but like the car business was showing me all business is about creativity, I wanted to buy and they wanted to sell, that's how I looked at it.

Together we could negotiate a deal. I called my farther in law Leon and discussed with him what I wanted to do; he told me that at this time he was paying the taxes on his properties that he was tight, so I said no problem. Teresita really wanted it and I wanted to give it to her. I told my wife he said no and she got a little depressed, because she wanted it more than me, I was happy at the Car dealership and saw myself growing. I went outside to my backyard and sat on a swing; I looked at the stars and said if this business is for us may it come to us, this is what I call quick! And conformation that the universe wanted me to have this business, Leon called me back that night and said I am not going to say yes! I'm not going to say no! Try and get them to lower their down payment. I might be able to do 10,000. I said thanks Leo that's all I need to negotiate with. I ask the owners to meet me at the Bakery I have an offer.

We all met at the bakery. I gave them my Offer, since it was credit, I gave them their price of 55,000, but the down payment would be 7,000 plus payments for 2 years with a balloon payment of 18,000 and 15,000 the year after. The husband thought about it, but the wife jumped and said "I am not selling you the business for less than $20,000 down" Like my customers did to me in the car business, I did to them. I shook their hand and said nice doing business with you. I turned around and started walking toward the door like I didn't care. 3 steps later the husband said do you have the 7,000 now? I said I could give you a certified check in 2 days. He told me sold!, the wife was pissed, but business is business. With the other 3,000 I turned on the lights, gas, insurance, phone, and food to sell, when all was set and done I had 100.00 dollars left, and with that I opened the new business.

The whole family working for no salary and 1 paid employee. This is not the best way to start a business, no working Capitol, just hope that the sales could pay the bills in time. Of course that would not happen so I sold my van for 2500 dollars to Colonial Chevrolet, so I could have some money to work with. That was still not enough, our first day we made 150.00 dollars, which was off my goal off 500.00.

The week before, I met Manny he was homeless and from NY he was visiting a friend in Virginia Beach, then wound up on the street because of an argument. I gave him a job and after a week of him working a brought him home and let him stay with us. He was young and had certain skills, I wanted to have around me, and He was a black belt and knew a lot about security. He was not as good a cook as he said he was, but his other skills allowed me to justify him working for me. He knew how to use weapons and taught my children martial arts. Manny did not look like a powerful karate Rambo type guy, he was short and husky and looked like a child, but he could twist you into a pretzel and then ask you, how you're doing. That impressed me. Manny told me his story and how he learned karate in the Bronx where he grew up. Law enforcement students, would go there for training, they liked him as a child so they trained him also with weapons and how to use them. He also knew the law. When you are in business you like to have people like that around you, protection is huge when you are carrying money, he could also protect my family. I kept my job at the dealership so after the first week I went back to work.

My wife was having a hard time by herself so I t quit my Job. BIG MISTAKE, now I had no extra income, no health benefits, nothing, just the cash register. I would be starting now my 3rd career. I started learning how to cook better then the woman we had working for us. My wife showed me also and I incorporated mine with theirs. Then I met Victor who owned a Puerto Rican Restaurant in Puerto Rico, he had opened one here but it failed. So he came to me for work and I gave it to him. He was interested in going into the Merchant Marines so I made him a deal. I help you get a job with MSC, you teach me how to cook Puerto Rican food, and he said deal. He taught me about seafood, Octopus, Conch, red snapper. Shrimp, mussels, paella, then the Rice, Pork, Chicken, beef, Beans, and plantains, green Banana, yucca, empanadas, I also had some ideas, but together I would become the chef of the family Restaurant and he got a job with my old company MSC. Life is great when people work together out of friendship, that is the true Puerto Rican, not some of the backstabbers I would meet in the future.

I started doing catering and my name started getting out there. I remember a certain big Hotel would order from me 500 empanadas for their banquets. I would vision in my mind trucks with El Latino Deli & bakery all over. I saw myself growing and helping the Latino community, my old friend Pedro who worked at the Recreation Center one day put together a Latin festival at the center. I donated roast Pork and *Arroz con gandules*, we were getting headlines in the papers and The Latino movement was going strong. We had Carlos on Saturday Nights playing Salsa out of Norfolk State University. We had Angel at Hampton University, various salsa groups were also in the area. and how could we forget "Willies" one of the first successful Latin Clubs in town. Then Tropicana would come later. The only problem I noticed was everybody had something negative to say about someone else. EGO, EGO, EGO, one time this woman came into my Bakery and told me That Puerto Rican food does not do well here, most restaurant go down in 6 months, I looked at her and said well I'm going to change that.

I was motivated by that in a way it lit a fire under me, you see I wasn't in business just to get rich; I was in business in order to keep my culture alive. When customers came in to eat and bring outside food for their kids, like pizza, or hamburgers, I would say! "hey what you doing" they would say that the food was too expensive to give the kids, so I would say throw away that junk, I would make a kids meal, cheaper than the outside fast food restaurants. I would say teach them to be Latino first then everything else second, here are American gringos learning Spanish and the culture, and enjoying our food and the ones with the culture not wanting it.

People that speak Spanish are getting extra money on their Jobs. I believe certain Latinos could be intimidated when surrounded by others who are not Latino, so they won't speak their native language. I got something funny to say here. The Civil War, Spanish, American War, WW1, WW2, all won by Immigrants from Italy, Ireland, Poland, Jewish, Puerto Rican, African, Mexican, and more, many soldiers didn't even speak proper English and they were all part of winning those wars. That's why I hate these idiots running around the country talking junk about immigrants, when it has always been the immigrants that has built this country. The only people who could complain about America are the real American, the red man.

We fight, complain, kill, destroy, and put ourselves through a living hell over a country stolen by our ancestors, instead of enjoying it. Let's be honest here who really busted their buts building this country? slaves. While the others puffed on Cigars.

I did my best running the business with whatever pennies I had and when going to get a loan I would be turned down. I would have to trust in my sales only, no loans for capitol, meanwhile as we burned American dollars fighting other country's problem, here in America we break our backs working and paying taxes for a Government that suppose to work for us, but they help their buddies who help them with campaign contributions. It's reverse capitalism. The Government makes mistakes than they tax you so they can overcome, but when you make one! You have to pay penalties, get your credit destroyed, and can't borrow a dime. What ever happen to a Government for the people? Republicans, and democrats, are like two babies and while they sit around playing Ego the rest of us are sitting around waiting for something good to happen. Losing our jobs, homes, businesses, no health care, is the real Star wars coming? are we are the rebels and the Government the evil Empire. I don't call Food stamps help! I call capitalism for all help.

The deadline first annual payment of 14,000 dollars was getting closer, but I had to borrow it from Leon. I was ashamed that he had to help me; I was married to his daughter 6 years and never needed any help until then. Something was telling me that the business was not a good idea, but I only remembered what the lady told me in the first few months I was open, that Puerto Rican restaurants don't last 6 months, I had already 1 year and for my anniversary I hired a DJ my friend Eddie. He did it for nothing a plate of *Arroz con Gandules con Carne Frita. Rice and beans with fried Pork* would be sufficient. I would give away free food, I set up a buffet of Puerto Rican food and whoever showed could have a plate. I had to market myself because Mexican food is what everybody knew. However I was always generous, even when I sold cars I could have been a 15 car a month guy, however I would always think of others, call it Equal capitalism all of us have the right to a good check. I would sell 10-11 make 3000. Or a little more than sit back and let others catch up. The rewards are always greater when one is fair and generous.

The year 2000 would come in, and all the talk of the end of the world like always was false. We were still here. I started doing more catering and meeting more people, we had our regulars, but we were still struggling. I was starting to get behind on the rent, my mortgage, credit Cards, food supply checks, bounced and the phone calls started coming in "High Mr. Garcia we just want to know when will receive the payment? "I will have it on Monday" ok thank you" It would be just like that. The payments for the bakery were killing me. I was giving the former owners 1500 a month which I never had, so they come and collect all the time or call me. I dealt with it and said to myself this will pass and all would be great. I was invited to be part of the Latin Festival that summer of 2000, I felt that the festival would help me get out of the hole it was El Latino deli& bakery, along with Guadalajara, that would be the sponsors.

I was the only food vender at the festival. It was crazy I did not know what I was doing, but I put it together and we made 2000 empanadas then froze them without putting paper in between them, so I lost a bunch of them because of that mistake, 1000 *alcapururias, Fried Pork, Tostones, Maduros,* and I also had Espresso coffee, and pastries *quesitos* and Guava. We made some good money, but we lost money also, because the setup was too costly and the food took too much prep hours. I lost more than I made, but inherited a lot of customers. I had lines outside my bakery the following week for lunch. Allot of catering orders and the final payment to the last owners was made. I was on a role. Since my Children worked for free all that time along with Manny who worked for room and board and family. I bought my oldest son a brand new truck, Andre was my right hand in the Business, Jeanette, and Leonell were my appetizers producers and Manny did security and watched my back. I would give Jeanette and Leonell some money and they go spend it at the mall. My wife and I were paying our mortgage and personal bills that satisfied us.

Chapter 9

The year 2000 was great and life was getting better, but we struggle at times. Every time the business looked like it was doing good rough times would come, I felt as something was always holding us back. We would never fall, but we would never grow. I should of walked away right there, most business people never fight a business they give it a couple of years then close or sell.

I remember our first one thousand dollar catering Job, it was a family reunion and they asked me to cater it. We had to be ready by 1230 pm, at red wing park in Va. Beach, myself and my son Andre got there on time. We set up the grill and the serving station with time to spare. I'm cooking and feeling great about myself, because I'm on time. Then my son tells me "hey dad" the name on this station is different from the name on the bill "I say what!! I look and say oh shit! We are setup up under the wrong tent. Chaos breaks out, and I start taking the food off the grill and telling my son hurry let's move this thing they will be here any moment. I lost it mentally and I'm blaming my poor son for my own failure to check the name on the tent. It was hot and humid, I'm trying to drag the grill across the field and almost caught a heart attack, my son got to the right station before me, so I am calling him like a nut waving my hand and fist saying "come over here and come help me" and of course cursing. We were able to get there before the people arrived and when they did. It looked like someone had thrown a bucket of water over me and my son looked delusional. The hamburgers were burned, and I had to go buy some more. We pulled it off though, we delivered the product, but it wasn't easy.

Another wild catering was the empanadas. A hotel in Virginia Beach ordered 500 empanadas, I was a little late, but I was on my way. I had them in aluminum pans, with aluminum foil covering them, out in front jumps another car. I slammed the breaks and there were empanadas, flying all over the front seat of the car, I'm telling you, the reason companies charge so much for catering is because the work that comes from preparing the catering and the Chaos you go through delivering it.

I was the most non expensive caterer in Hampton roads and people would still complain about the price. One lady asked me if I removed the *Gandules* from the rice would the rice be cheaper. I would cook for 100 people and get 500 dollars for *pernil, arroz con gandules*, potato salad, service, when the going rate was a minimum 15 a person. When I got married in 1984 for cold cuts, service, and salad I paid $2500.

That's the way I did business, if you came with a sad story, I would try and accommodate you. I did have my good catering jobs where, I would get paid well, not all were cheap. I guess, I was a bad business man. I could never tell a person no, I always said no problem. I loved the way I was surrounded by Puerto Ricans all the time that was the real profit the people and the culture. I saw woman who were having babies eating my food and pastries, I saw their children grow and witnessed them walking and talking from the beginning. I remember Kimberly she was 15 when she come with her mother and brother. Years later she worked for me. I saw her children grow and eat my food and pastries also. Puerto Ricans who had family here would come from the island to live here and some would come to me for work, and I would help them and give them a job. I did not have a restaurant; I had a community center and was following my dad's footsteps being a leader in my community. My children would work for no money while others work and got paid. I would tell my kids don't worry this will pay off one day. I also remember this guy he was very funny he would come into the bakery and say *dame todo que engorda* "he said give me everything that makes you fat.*

The bad thing about Hampton roads is people come and go, sometimes you meet good people but they are only here for 1 year or less and you lose them.

We started making cakes for people so my son would be in charge of that department. One day he made a cake for a customer, I told him it was too tall and it was going to fall apart, he would not listen, so here comes the lady to pick up her cake, she likes it and says "yummy" she pays us and my son tells her to hold the cake in a certain way, ok says the customer. El Latino Deli front was all windows so you could see the customers coming from the parking lot, about 10 minutes later here comes this poor girl with her cake. It looked like it exploded. I just took money out of the register plus an additional 20 dollars and said I'm very sorry" "she said don't worry, I will get a cake somewhere else. So my son comes up to me and says "I told her she had to hold it in a certain way." We would argue, but I let it go. I then put the broken cake at the counter, and us Puerto Ricans are something else, one guy took a piece and says "man this cake taste good" and when the rest knew it was free they all got some, one guy said, "call that girl back it looks ugly but it taste good." One guy gave 3.00 dollars and took the rest home.

The real Puerto Rican always turns adversity into triumph or a good joke, the ones that don't are the ones you call converted Jerk off Puerto Ricans. The people who think they are better.

The military also became a great asset to me, every year on September 15, to October15, was Latino month. My name got around quickly and I had at least 30 catering jobs going. I would bring food on the base, before I opened the doors of El Latino. I already had 500.00 dollars so another 500.00 was 1 thousand and that was a very good day for our family. I would send Andre to pick up Leonell, and Jeanette, from school so they could help; all three kids were always in the bakery.

I remember Jeanette complaining that her education was being put on hold, because she was always in the bakery. Jeanette was me in a lot of ways. I would love to hear her moan and groan, but I didn't care, "get your butt to the bakery" I would say. I need Quesitos, Gauva, pastries, Flan tres Leche. Leonell was my empanada, man he could make 100 of them in 1 hour. Manny would also help, but would eat more then he would help. They all deserved a lot for the work they did without pay. On Saturdays we did well and I pay them 30 dollars each, and I give Andre 50 dollars, and they would all say yahoo. On Sundays I would take them out to eat and go to the Mall, Jeanette would be broke 2 minutes in the mall, but I would still help her and the others if they went overboard, and we also catch a movie, me and Teresita did a great Job raising our Children. When guys try to call home for Jeanette and I pick up the phone they would hang up. I was very strict with her and her friends. I wanted my children to make sure they have a great life and enjoyed it.

I would always talk to them about alcohol, drugs, and gangs. I explained to them what had happen to me, and I would teach them how to keep an inventory of themselves. Later on that year my farther in law would be diagnosed with cancer and my wife would go to Puerto Rico back and forth. I then took take care of the kids and the business, Teresita was very close to Leon, and she started to suffer, we all did. Leon was more than my farther in Law he was my best Friend. I call him almost every day when I was cooking something in the restaurant. I would call him and say "Leon I'm making some *Mondongo*, He say I'm going to open my mouth pass it through the phone. I would say "ok Leo" he it comes" he would say "it taste good, but it needs salt." I would laugh and we have a great time. The funny thing is when I met him in 1997 when Teresita was still married to Andy we got along great back then. Life is full of surprises, you never know the people you meet how they could become such a great impact on your life. I was praying a lot for him.

When I was in the business my spiritual walk had stopped. I prayed watched myself continue to go to alcohol support groups, but I wasn't meditating or reading anymore. I would write in my journal 2-3 months at a time, when I used to do it every day. My attitude did not change, but I was getting angry again because the business just took up all of my time, worry, worry, worry, money was the only thing on my mind. I would only think of how to pay the bills. My house was falling apart because the business would always take all the income. No bank would give me a loan, then911 happen. I still remember that day I went to open the store and while I was cooking my wife calls me in a worried voice saying "TYRONE WE ARE BEING ATTACKED" I said by who? She said I don't know, then I said when you find out let me know, but I'm making Rice and Beans right now so let me be. Next door there was a barber shop with a television, I saw people walking up and looking from the outside and when I checked I saw the twin towers burning and watched the 2nd plane hit that was really something. I felt bad for the people who lost their lives no one should express their political views with murder. I don't care how pissed you are, it was a cowardly act.

That is a touchy subject so I will pass on that one, though it would hurt our economy because Bush Junior decided to turn it into a war that would last too long. In 1986 President Reagan sent the battle ship New Jersey to Libya dropped a few bombs and left, in 1991 Bush Sr. sent the military to Kuwait and liberated them and left but Jr. got to turn it into Viet Nam. Break the country over it, and we are still over there, spending millions while Americans are working for 7.25 an hour. What is wrong with this picture? The war would empty out the bases and a lot of my customers gone. Another problem in Hampton Roads for business owners, no military no money, when the military came to me for catering they would come with less and less money every year. I would do it, but what I don't understand is they are coming to me with 150.00 dollars to buy food for 50 people, but giving the Iraqis millions of our tax dollars, for what? Iraqis weren't even involved in 9-11" The other funny thing is during the Iraq and Iran war we supported Sadaam Husien now he is our enemy why? The Bush administration was very weird. I voted for him which even made it worse.

My wife would go back to Puerto Rico, and I go with her, but I came back and she would stay. Leon was getting worse and she cared for him and her mother Ana. I was ok with Teresita helping her dad and me holding down the fort, but the Vultures were out, hey Tyrone where is your wife? oh she is taking care of her dad, oh she has been gone a long time" I was starting to get angry because people could get a little too personal and I know exactly what they were trying to say. I started just staying in the back of the bakery so I wouldn't have to be interrogated by our customers. The business started to hurt more and even when I had a good week the following week would be bad. I was falling behind on my rent, mortgage, car, I would pay my utility bills 1 day before the cutoff date it was rough. I would look at the sales to see if we could pay our bills. The problem was, we try to pay them as the sales came in. I started with only 100.00 dollars. I recall when I started this business they were no Government money involved in the purchase of the business. I'm telling you the Government could be worse than the mob when you owe them money. I learned a lot about the government while in business, but that is the way it is. The supplier is another one, I will tell you one episode, I owed this supplier some money. I was putting it together for him, but it was taking me a few days he comes by and says just give me a check and I will deposit it on Monday" I say I might not have it till Wednesday, so he deposit the thing and bounces about 4 other checks at 35 dollars a whop. Then he tells me hey Tyrone your check bounced. I said I told you, "I could give you all the checks you want I have plenty what I don't have is money to cover it.

He was very angry and said "well I coming for cash next time. I said ok. I would pay him the cash, but the other supplier deposits his check and since I couldn't keep my plan, that one bounces and another 35 dollars. Now I'm supporting the bank for doing nothing. The bank asks me hey Tyrone you need overdraft protection, I said yes give me that, oh we are sorry but your credit isn't good enough. You could put a 1000.00, dollars in the account and that will help you not go over, in that moment you just want to slap the shit out of this moron. Oh my God!! What the hell did I get into? What happen to the great American Dream were we could get some money from the bank to stock our shelves and do business. I was witnessing the Great American nightmare. The business was doing 10,000-12000 a month, but I would have almost 400 dollars in bank fees alone from being forced to pay and hoping the sales were on time, but it would never happen. I was losing my mind. I needed a loan just 12,000 dollars so I could pay my bills and save my sales for next month, so I could get ahead. It was just a constant battle, but guess what! This Puerto Rican never closed, and I kept going and dealing with it, a Puerto Rican family in Virginia working and not being able to pay their bills or even have health Insurance, but we never gave up, I felt that I would see the light. Watch who you call lazy!! This Puerto Rican family was not, and we didn't ask for you freaking welfare or Medicaid. I was being told that my kids could have gotten Medicaid, but I told them If you think I'm going to give some racial jerk off; the benefit of looking at me, like I'm here for his welfare, I rather live in pain, when we have a medical problem. Though I would get some insurance it would last for awhile, but then it would lapse because we didn't make the payment.

Small business struggles a lot they always have to find their own money in order to operate. Nobody cares about them, I always knew what the problem was, however I could never get a loan. I remember being with First Bank of Va. I talked to a man about a loan he came from Downtown Norfolk and we talked, but I didn't get a dime. I had some other representatives come to me and before even putting in an application I was denied. That was BB&T the same bank, just merger. I came to the conclusion that I would have to do this myself along with my family and hopefully my clients. I was invited to sell food at the New Latin Fest which would be my second one. The first one was organized by the Multi Cultural Organization which was Angel Morales. He is no longer with us, may he rest in peace. He did so much for the Latin community a retired US Army officer. He was also a great friend of mine and helped me a lot, and also catered from me, always representing in the Community.

Hampton roads had many Latino's trying to bring up the community. The local Spanish teachers would order Cuban Sandwiches from me, and bring in the students, turning my restaurant into a Spanish class. Which would also bring me customers, the Latino Community was giving me a lot of love, and in return I made sure I stay open so they could have a place they could say was theirs. You also had the bad one's the people who was envious, the haters who don't like seeing their own people grow. I call them the" lost souls of America" they have been smacked around and never seen nothing but grief, they like to share it with you and never have nice thing to say, always complaining and always putting down the people in their race, acting very negative.

I once threw out a customer because he was talking bad about Puerto Rico, It was during the bombing of Vieques, in Puerto Rico was tired of it. A security Guard while on duty was killed during military operations, there were signs of frustration from Puerto Ricans and the Navy threatened to leave which had certain PRs angry. Me myself I believed at the time that America, was showing it's true colors, they can complain as Americans but we can't, the constitution of the US states is just for certain people only. All of a sudden the bad blood starts, "get rid of them" we support them" they are all on welfare'" the island isn't worth it." Our tax dollars supports them while they stay home and sleep and I work. My Bakery would turn into a debate more than a bakery. I stood with my mouth open listening to PR talking about their people and the island. Meanwhile they complain in Virginia Beach, about Jet noise, but it's ok to bomb Vieques. This is what they are really saying "hey you fucking spics shut up we support you" I was born and raised in this country, and I know it well. Don't get me wrong I have many American friends that I would go to war for, but we still have some rotten apples in the core that need to be dealt with, if we are to have any peace and prosperity amongst us all . . . . Nobody is going anywhere, we are here for the long haul, and the way some countries are aligning themselves with others, America is going to need all the help it can get.

Puerto Ricans since 1898 have been owned by the US. Puerto Ricans who live on the island can't vote for the President, however, we have fought in every major war the US has had since WW 1 and have been drafted to. That is loyalty at is best. In the Viet Nam war Puerto Ricans were getting drafted off the island to fight for a country that called them spics and didn't allow the island PRs to vote, while certain Americans were escaping to Canada, and burning the American flag at the colleges, my cousin Toni went to Viet Nam he didn't even speak English that good, I remember him, he was in the Marines and retired an E-8 he lives in North Carolina.

Why must we deal with racism? We have to hear racial slurs from ignorant Americans; if in 114 years we have not gotten any respect then maybe it is time to depart. This is not my call; I am only reacting to what I see that's all. Well that would go on at the Bakery for a year and when the Navy left I said low blow, but, Puerto Rico finally won a fight, that was more of a victory then a lost. Pedro Albizu Campo, smiled and the heavens were full of light, I'm honored that the Navy created Jobs for Puerto Ricans, but at the price of Cancer from the radiation coming from Bombs I'd rather pick bananas.

My farther in law was told his cancer was at a level 4 and we all knew he would not last. on June 3, 2002 he called me. It was my tenth year of Sobriety and he said," what would you do if I told you, you hit the lottery" I knew what he was going to say, I knew that he was going to tell me his time was coming to an end, and was about to offer me one of his properties. He told me that he was leaving me and his Daughter a paid off property in Puerto Rico It was the property where he started his business, and upstairs had an apartment. It was a 3 bedroom apartment upstairs, store front downstairs a barber shop and a machine shop in the back. It had 2 entrances one on the left side of the street and one on the other side. It would give me and Teresita a net worth of 300.000 thousand dollars, In Real estate. He said do what you want with it, rent it, or sell it, whatever it takes to fix your financial problems. The bank will respect you now. You have been a great son to me. As much as I wanted to jump up and down I couldn't' you see Leon was like my spiritual friend that I could talk to, we had great conversations together, for many years. I could just not see him go. A couple of days later, I put on this Indian regalia I made along with my son Andre. I burned some sage and tried to get the cancer out of him through strong spiritual dance and prayer, meditation. I just tried to do everything I can to take the cancer in myself. Then fly it out to the universe and blow it away so we could all be happy. I tried so hard, but I am not God. I would fly to Puerto Rico in July and be with my old friend Leo for the last time. He didn't talk much and he wasn't the same, but I had a remedy.

I told him the story about the time I sent my dad a check in order to help him, and forgot to transfer the funds and the check bounced. Leo would laugh allot at that story so I figure I cheer him up. My dad's comments after he learned of the bad check was, "Dear son don't try to help me anymore with money it cost me 35 dollars to accept your help" That would make Leo laugh no matter how bad he felt. That was very funny to him and every time I shared it with him he laugh. Leon died on Friday August 23, 2002 at 1230 pm, In San Juan Puerto Rico. I was at the Bakery, my wife called me and told me that I needed to stay at the bakery, because it was going to be quick plus the business was in trouble and the money wasn't available to fly. I told my son Andre clean up and close early, we will close for 1 day for mourning. I close my room door and act like Leo was right there, and I would talk to him. I would call his house so I could hear his voice on the message machine. I had lost a great human being someone who knew how to listen without criticizing.

My wife would become depressed. She really loved her dad and spent almost 2 years with him while he suffered, and me with nothing, but honor would take care of the kids and the business while she was over in Puerto Rico. The property would take a while before we can get it so we continue to struggle. My wife stood in Puerto Rico in order to help her Mother, but I was getting a little restless because 2 months have gone by. I traveled to Puerto Rico and brought her back.

In November of 2002, my brother Angelo was giving 6 months to live because of his cancer, liver cancer. He was the brother that helped me while I was struggling, and took me to rehab and also would look for me when I was on my three day benders. He was thinking of coming to Virginia Beach to go into business with me. I will travel numerous times to New York to visit him and I was saying what in the hell is happening. He was looking pretty bad and I said I'm losing my close family members. I still had my other 2 brothers Jose, and Jimmy, and My sister Maritza.

Maritza husband was in the Army so they were always traveling along with my lovely nieces, and nephews, Marili, Marisita, Papipito, Jimmy, and Alexi. We would always travel to see my sister when they were living in Aberdeen proving grounds Maryland Army base. Marisita was the oldest of my sister kids, and the one who took on the role of playing the second mother while my sister was working. Marili was the little actor who was always dancing. She would say look Uncle Tyrone check this move out. I knew that one day she would become an actress, which she is today. Alexis was the cute little girl you wanted to kiss every time you saw her. Papito was also a very good boy who would ask many questions and today is in the Air Force. Jimmy was another good boy and loved football and a Raven fan; he is also in the Air Force. Jorge the dad well he is what you call the Real Puerto Rican loves his beer, can fix anything, the best host whenever you visit him along with his guitar. He retired from the Army. My Sister is the enemy she works for the IRS. I call her the Government. My kids and my sister's kids would grow up together in different areas, but we kept in touch.

Angelo was irreplaceable there was nobody like Angelo he was funny and had this enormous energy to work. He worked for the City Morgue, he also drove a Funeral limo, and had his wife run a little discount store, he would work there after his shift, and would volunteer to talk to troubled kids in a juvenile facility. He couldn't keep a secret neither, he tell mom everything he knew and make her laugh. Angelo when picking up a corpse on a call one day saw that the dead woman had a nice watch on. He decided to take it and give it to my mother. My mother asks where he gets it from. And He says "off the dead woman I have downstairs in the meat wagon" she says what!! My mother screamed! She tried to take the watch off and couldn't. she tell, Angelo please take it off! "Mom" Angelo says . . . The woman is dead she doesn't need it anymore. My mother did not keep it and since the dead woman was in the meat wagon downstairs, while Angelo stop for some coffee and give a dead gift to my mom, he says "I put it back on the corpse arm" no respect for the dead. That was Angelo; pretty twisted.

When Angelo was 7 years old he was hit by a car and wasn't supposed to survive. my mother went to the church, and said a prayer, she says she didn't care about the life Angelo was going to have just don't let him die. When my mother got back to the room Angelo was moving around like nothing happen to him. He would at adult age go to Jail twice. Mom would witness the same thing I witnesses, before me, seeing your son get handcuffed and taking off to jail. I would go visit him with my other brother Jose. When I went there I saw a lot of Puerto Ricans and black and some whites it was Prison. I hate to say it this way, but what did Puerto Ricans see in America that was worth all the shit we put up with. My farther tells me that Puerto Rico was a great place to live until, Puerto Ricans started sending their kids back to Puerto Rico so they could change, because they were becoming gangsters in New York all they did was bring the American ghetto mentality to Puerto Rico and destroy it.

I remember when parents would say to the kids when they kids were getting bad habits "I'm sending you back to PR with your aunt so I don't lose you". We all know today how that went. No matter what, there is a solution, but I will discuss that in my finale. My brother Angelo died on Friday, May 23rd at 3pm 2003 In the Bronx New York. I had lost 2 great people in less than a year. I was able to go to my brother's funeral I drove to the Bronx and bumped into a lot of people I grew up with in Bronx River. Many people came to see Angelo; he had a big Funeral just the way he wanted.

We would go back to Virginia and start focusing on what we were going to do. Two doors down from me they opened this beautiful Argentine Restaurant. They were not doing so good, but I liked the way they built their restaurant. If I could only get that restaurant, it would make me the first Puerto Rican owned full service restaurant with 5 years experience. It had a little dance floor with a wall designed as a Spanish town. The kitchen was small and it didn't have facilities for baking, But I assured myself we find a way, it also had a 17 chair lighted up bar with 2 large mirrors and lots of colors, it was nice and I wanted it for my customers. I know it would be a great success, I expected them to get restless and see if they would sell . . . It was the summer and I did my 4th Latin Festival like always. The line was long and the sales were jumping. I go today to these festivals and never here one thing about how we were one of the pioneers of the Latin Fest, well God knows and that's all who needs to know. The owners of the restaurant visited me several times, but I did not budge, because I had no money to offer. I needed to wait for the lawyer In Puerto Rico to call me. He would let me know when I could get the property that was left to me and Teresita. We were going to sell the property in Puerto Rico, because the area were the property was—was getting bad so I had no interest in doing business there plus Leo had a for Sale sign for awhile already, so I left the sale sign, however I would learn about Puerto Rican Politics, and business in the worse way.

Chapter 10

The lease on the space I was renting for the business would be up for renewal In February of 2004. I was thinking of selling or just walking away and enjoying what I had, the new property in Puerto Rico, 70,000 was owed on my house in Va. Beach with over 85,000 worth of equity I was sitting on 400.000 dollars in properties with a paid off business that was iffy and needed capitol. I would have to really think about my next move.

The restaurant next to me was selling, and I felt I could take it into a profitable direction. I wondered if I was just doing it to make money or continue running my community center! I remember how certain customers were happy that I had the restaurant and when family from Puerto Rico came to visit they will want to go to El Latino for conversation and food, a tradition I added to the bakery.

Latino people love to socialize when eating or drinking coffee. Only in America coffee has become a get it quick and go to work place. I talked with my wife about the property in Puerto Rico we discussed what we wanted to do and decided to go along with the purchase of the bigger restaurant. She called the Lawyer and asked him when could we take possession of the property? The lawyer said by March of 2004, so I called a bank in Puerto Rico HF mortgage and spoke to a representative called Rosaline Veneges, she told me how much money she could help me with, but needed certain documents. I was doing business with a bank in Puerto Rico with my Spanish, at times I had to rephrase myself because she wouldn't understand my Spanglish, but I tried and we got a good relationship going with the Bank. I was going to borrow money from a bank in Puerto Rico so my Restaurant was PURO PUERTORRIQUENO!!!. No thanks to Hampton Roads and there bank system which to me every person I talked to had no clue of doing business.

Restaurant owners get no respect only when you become successful and don't need any loans is when they talk to you. Well I had everything set and all I needed was time to think. The owners would ask me from time to time if I had made up my mind, and I would answer. "Still thinking" I was told to wait to see if they would fold, but they had deep pockets, and Leon always told me to be an honest business man, always pay what is worth to you. If you had to do the same, allow the seller to be able to walk away with something, because it may happen to you one day. I would go in and look at the equipment, construction, everything, the place was brand new they were asking for $125.000 cash. I would go home and think about it and wait a week. I than answered them and offered 65.000 dollars, credit for 5 Months, starting January of 2004 with a onetime payment of 65,000 in May 2004. This was in November 2003. He said deal. I would take over the rent in January which was my negotiation; in addition to that the landlord gave me 1 free month of rent, so rent wouldn't be due till February. He would give me the key in January 3rd 2004.

I remember how Leon would tell me to always take short, solid, steps, well that would become a long unstable step, because I was doing business with no money, just with my gut feeling. My house had the equity, but my credit was pretty bad, however the bank in Puerto Rico didn't care! My property was all I needed for the loan; along with my word that I would pay off some of the bad loans. That makes more sense than the garbage the banks In Va. Beach were telling me. I had a home with equity, but still could not get the help I needed to fund My business, if you look at my business, I was doing well, however, when paying from behind your 12,000 a month is more like 6,000 a month, because of late fees, overdraft fees, all these great things the banks do to you, so you're not late again, which really is how they get over on you, and keep you down in the gutter so you can't overcome. Banks are nothing but bullies they only bend when they see large capital reserves in your business, but, when asking for help they tell you very simple go screw yourself.

I'm going to tell you how stupid some banks are in this area. I walked into a bank with $18.000 dollars to pay off El Latino Deli& bakery, and instead of the bank manager asking me what I intend to do with that money? I deposit it and made a certified check to the couple who sold me the business. Here is what I would of done "hello Mr. Customer: my that's is a large deposit you are making, how is your business doing? Oh this money is to pay it off the people who sold me the business. "Oh I see" but that would leave your business account at 100.00. How about this? "I will loan you the 18.000 say at 6% and you could freeze the 18.000 dollars" and as you pay I will release" That will allow your corporation to pay it off in 3 to 5 years." The 18.000 will be available to you If you don't use it" and I will give you 2% interest on your 18.000 dollars" so it's really 4%. That will allow you to capitalize on the $18.000 plus help your credit grow with us. If you struggle to make the payment we could just take the 18.000 or what's left.

Instead what did I get, some lady with the take out Chinese menu telling me she can't help me. I wonder why Americans are not capitalizing. We depend on a computer not research on the customer; why even have bank personal when the machine does everything. That was one of the banks that were bailed out by our tax dollars in 2008; I will keep their name anonymous. The capitalism that is practiced is to destroy and conquer not to help and bring abundance toward everybody.

Here it goes; you are late with a payment, because you are swimming in a whirlpool of debt, but you see you can get out, but they add a stronger whirlpool so they could continue greasing you for money. Then when you're tapped out they come and take everything you worked hard for your home, car, credit, everything just like a mafia bust out, on someone's business that couldn't pay the bookie. The Government is no different they do it with the Law protecting them. The Government, local, and federal, has destroyed more American families with back taxes than anything else; it's unbelievable how they get away with it.

I believe at one time taxes were a contribution to the state how did this get out of hand so quick. So I could support some guy who doesn't have a job? Well America get him a dam job and let me keep my money I'll help you, but don't drain me. I believe in Government services we do need them, what I don't believe is how does a country with so much area, vegetation, land, and a high demand for products don't have a job for everyone. Why are old people working at supermarkets instead of enjoying their golden years ah! Our society is really full of shit . . . We have tons of problems in America and immigration is not one of them! If it wasn't for immigrants I wouldn't be able to drink orange Juice in the morning. The problem is? We create more problems for people then they can handle, we keep sinking our country with hate and greed and creating more greedy companies that make billions for themselves and little for the ones who work and help them make those billions. At the end we will wind up with a country full of broke people. That is what I foresee in the future greedy capitalism is like the game Pac-man, if any of you remember, it just eats away everything in sight until there's nothing left, and then it will eat itself.

I believe in capitalism, I feel we should all be able to capitalize on anything we want, but, within reason not where we companies ship jobs overseas and leave Americans hanging without a job, and still want tax loopholes and tax breaks. Or the Government having to bail out people who only care about them, and don't want to pass some on the profits to create more abundance and profits for others . . . there is enough to go around, but, what is enough? How many Americans are scared to go to the mailbox or check their e-mail, well I went through living hell in business, however, I did not run to the Government for help which I could have used, but I didn't? I had no Medicaid no nothing, nada; I told my kids, don't get sick. I believe in regulations on how and where you build your business. I feel it's unfair that we have super stores like Wallmart, they have over 20 or more different businesses within! How about selling cars also, Why not sell vacations, insurance, hell buy up all the real estate and sell that to. Monster retail stores that have many types of business within kill small business.

I like walmart, his story is great and I have a great deal of respect for the family, however when your parking lot is so full and everybody else is empty it's not fair. The scariest business is the one that eats up everything and others go under because they can't compete.

The year was coming to an end I promised the kids and staffs a trip to Disney world in December, every December 24th I would do the Christmas dinner 1 pork shoulder. Rice with Beans, Pasteles, and bread for 89.99, It would feed a family of 8. I would sell 30 to 40 dinners and spend it on the hard working staff of mine. My wife and 3 children plus many, Andre's future wife Jackie and whoever was the dishwasher which that year was Panama Jeanette's boyfriend. Like always the dinner went well. I rented a nice Cadillac and my son drove the Monte Carlo, I rented a house in Orlando Florida with a pool in the back 5minutes from Disney. We drove right after I sell the last Dinner. We close up the store people already knew we closed every year from the 25th to the Jan 2.

I loved taking vacation all at the same time. Some people would get mad because we were closed, my complain is what's the sense of working yourself to death, everybody deserves a vacation even business owners. That's another problem in this country we work too much, then when we are old we are fighting disease or cancer. Then who enjoys your hard earned money the funeral, hospital, and Lawyer. Leon told me whenever you could take a vacation take it because you don't know when it would be your last. One must enjoy his royalties even if they are small so when you go to work you go with passion not the, "ah not work again attitude" which is the worse karma you could bring into any retail business. If you came to work for me with negative energy I would send you home in my next chapter I would speak more about the characters.

We had a great time in Orlando we went to all the parks and got on the rides we enjoyed the pool and just let go of the stress of working in a restaurant; especially El Latino Deli. The air condition unit didn't supply us with enough cool air so the summer was over 95 degrees in there. The Bakery had 4 ovens going all the time baking, making roast Pork, then the burners cooking rice and beans. The staff really deserved a good vacation. We get back to Virginia and my stomach started getting the butterflies, why? I owed money and now the rent for both places were due, I took care of one of them because I remembered the rental office gave me 1 free month so I did not pay in late February I was giving a note by the landlord saying I was behind on the new location. I told him that I was giving a free month. All new leases get a free month. March came and me and my wife flew to Puerto Rico so we could get our loan, the bank was ready but, the papers weren't, my God there was still a lot of things to do; so here it goes, In Puerto Rico everything is done slow pace I needed to go to departamento De Hacienda, which is the tax Department to get a document, but first we had to go to the Crim which is another tax department, and get these stamps that cost thousands of dollars. We didn't have much money so my mother in law Ana lend us the money in order to get the ball rolling.

I visited our new building and started cleaning it up and putting some money into it. I offered to rent it cheap 950.00 a month for the bottom part only, but I wanted 2 months in advance so I found someone and with that same money bought materials so I could get the building going. I quickly talked to the people in the area and started to learn who was who. Doing business in Puerto Rico is no difference than any other place, but in Puerto Rico nobody is working through lunch, people eat when it's time to eat. I also found someone to rent for 300.00 a month a little piece were they gamble on the horse races. In order to get the loan I needed some local income, so I got some renters. I really did my homework and proving to myself that I was truly a business man.

When the bank appraised the building it came back light $200.000 I blew up and called Rosaline, she gave me the name of the appraisers and I went and with my "Spanglish" got them to up it 50,000 dollars! I don't know if I scared the guy or when I gave him some other measurements he saw his mistake, but the appraisers changed the numbers. I told my wife I think I could really handle Puerto Rico Here I am a nyorican ex junkie alcoholic no education doing business with Puerto Rico's business sector, and picked up $50.000 doing it.

My son Andre 25, was at the restaurant running it along with Manny26 and Jeanette, 18, Leonell 15 those were the ages of my Kids when I left them in charge. The time was running and bills were mounting up the rent was behind, my car payment, my mortgage, and taxes. My kids were not cooking that great and they pretty much couldn't handle the bakery. I knew what was going to happen, but I also knew I needed to get this done. It was just a matter of time, but March would pass and the paperwork I was waiting for from the Government of Puerto Rico was taking too long. By mid April the relief paper showed up and now the Lawyer had to add all this language to it that would take 3 weeks. By the 3rd week of April the landlord had locked up the Bakery and the new location for default of payment. My son called me and said the landlord allowed us to clean up and while cleaning we took home some food, now I was in constant contact with the landlord and my lawyer in Puerto Rico send him a letter stating to them we were waiting on legal papers, their money was coming, but he still put the locks on and a sign for lease. I felt like the biggest fool in the world. I could see the haters just laughing at me and my children what am I going to do? However God is great! My son Andre got a Job at a fish market, Jeanette did some Babysitting and Manny got a Job at seven eleven and they all watched Leonell. THIS IS A PUERTO RICAN FAMILY IM TALKING ABOUT my children took the initiative to take care of themselves they said dad we got it under control you take care of business, after a long cry of worry on a bench in Guaynabo Puerto Rico, I went to work. I painted my wife aunts house and she paid me. I would get the rent on the first of May.

I made a deal with the new renters who were selling food; I rented them the upstairs apartment for an additional 400.00 which bought 3 bedrooms and terrace. I was then collecting enough money in rent to pay the new mortgage. By mid may the lawyer finished so it had to go back and be redone all over again, but with our names on the deed, this is the killer! I was the only food vender for the Latin festival on June 4th and it was already May 15th the other thing was my brother in law band from Puerto Rico was going to play in the Latin Fest, I had gotten that setup with Leo who was the man who would book the bands. I remember Pipo talked about how one day he would love to play on the beach with his group. Well I got him his wish, something I take seriously; I love to make things happen for people. I believe when a person shares with you their dreams you should always pray that they get it. I stood pretty cool and just prayed every day that all would go well and we get this money and go back home.

A trip that was suppose to last 1 week, lasted 3months, by late May we would get the proper documentation in order to get the loan. I called Rosaline and she said great! bring that paper and we are on our way. 3 days later we closed on the deal, in a bank in Hato Rey. I would get my first loan for my business in Puerto Rico. It was 92,000 dollars the payment was 900 a month the property was bringing some money to pay the loan for the first year. I was a capitalist! Thanks to my best friend and farther in law Leon. When flying back to the United States I just looked at the check I never thought the day would come I see my name on a check so big even though it was a loan it was really my money because it was credited from our property. I couldn't wait to deposit it in the bank.

I had my business account with BB&T. Sharon was the best person who worked there she was the manager. When I got to Va. Beach I went to the bank, I was giving 25.000 quick as Sharon knew I needed it, I made a check for back rent and went to the landlord and said can I have my keys! I told you I would be back here's your money. He gave me the keys and Tereisita's Latino Bar & grill was born. Though the corporate name would still be EL Latino deli & bakery, I then would lend the money to the corporation. God helps us but we must do the leg work! no good deed goes unpaid." I may looked like a fool, but know I look l like a hero, because I did not allow anything to stop me, my culture would continue to live on the corner Of Holland and South Plaza Trail. With the financial help of Puerto Rico, Leonides Vargas, and of course how can I forget Rosaline, gracias?"

My experience of the last 5 years was this? Running a business was no different than the business I learned on the street's growing up. People are out to help you, some are out to get over on you, and some are envious of your success. Success brings enemies. I noticed how some Puerto Ricans were always being negative about what I was doing; it would anger me to witness that. When El Latino deli opened in 1998, I would go and by food from them and was proud that there was a place I could hang my hat, and meet with Puerto Ricans and other Latino people, It's what I loved the most about it, and that is why I kept it going.

I would experience people coming to my bakery and complaining about the Prices of the other restaurant, "El San Juan" I couldn't believe how they cried so much about the prices on the menu. I already had the tissue on the table so they could wipe their tears. They would say," I had Rice and Beans and Roast Pork they charged me 12 dollars" I would also hear the same complains. I struggled throughout my time there. If it wasn't for Leon giving me that property in order to expand, I would have lost it all.

On the plane ride back, I thought of taking that 92.000 dollars and paying off my home in Va. Beach which would have left me 25.000 and a new start. I could have gone back to the car dealership and had $250.000 of equity in Puerto Rico, $195.000 in equity in Va. Beach, and my own home with no mortgage to pay that is almost a half a million dollars in addition to receiving rent payments from the property in Puerto Rico.

I only vision the people eating and having a place to speak Spanish and enjoy their culture. I would rule in favor of happiness for the people even though it would enslave me to a shaky business. Given the landlord the money and proving I wasn't making it up was also more important for me. I decided to put the money into the business and open Teresita's Latin Grill. I would hire my son Andre and send him to Bartending School. I hired Jackie his wife my younger son Leonell, as for Jeanette, I had to sweet talk her back and she accepted to work in the new restaurant. But said, I want to get paid, and she would. I setup payroll with a company called Paychex, and they did a very good job. My daughter would be head waitress, My wife the host, Me the chef, I hired panama, for dishwasher and salads, Leonell, in the kitchen with me and Manny was working somewhere else, but he would come by from time to time. He decided to work security.

My other waitress was a girl who from the age of 14 was eating at the Deli with her mom Kimberly, and Mirta, the Daughter of Jose who were long time customers also. That was the team we started with. I would later get Joanna, and Suhaley, as waitresses. Desserts were flan, vanilla custard, Three milk cake, Tembleque, Guava Pastries, Quesitos, all made by Jackie who we taught, an African American woman from Florida was making Puerto Rican Deserts and all the customers loved it. I made my famous Roast Pork which was the signature dish, Churrasco, skirt steak, Grilled chicken breast with a special sauce I would create, NY strip steaks, Fried pork, sautéed shrimp in garlic, butter, white wine and spices, Mofongo, Rice and Beans, empanadas and much more.

The place on its first day was packed and we made over 1000 dollars we were not use to that type of daily sales, before we were making like 300-400 a day in the Bakery. It was like we opened the gates of heaven because without any advertising the place filled with old and new customers happy to see us back. That night I said, it was worth spending the 92,000 dollars on the new business. We made mistakes, but were able to overcome them, we started getting more of the locals yes the gringos were coming in by the packs for my roast Pork and Cuban sandwiches, and our big time local Lawyer friend Bob, which in my book is the best Lawyer in town, in heart and spirit. "Cuban sandwich with extra pickles" was his order. The locals were becoming regulars and I was getting catering jobs from them. Our customer base was diverse something I needed in order to be successful. Teresitas Grill was growing our monthly sales went from 12.000 a month to 27.000, a month, my taxes were paid and all was flying high.

I was paying everybody, hey, I was getting a paycheck also we had health insurance, It was the right decision all was going great, Thanks to the generous help of my friend and in law Leonides Vargas RIP.

We lost some customers, because I had to raise my prices in order to capitalize on my investment, plus I made sure the cooperation paid me back every month the money I had lend in order to make this happen.

We invented the "hot corner", with Jose, Frankie RIP, Linda, Crissy, Lee, Donald, Tony, and many more. I started "Social Fridays," Social Fridays is a Puerto Rican tradition whereas the people start partying early Friday. It would carry over into Saturday night. I would make special dishes from Puerto Rico for them. The salsa music was going and the place was electric.

I was giving a plaque and an article from the Virginia pilot that said Puerto Rico at the Beach. I also won best of the beach In Latin food category, over all the Mexican restaurants and that banner was on the front with Puerto Rican pride. I was enjoying the new place, because people were coming in and loving the place and food. Spanish teacher's, from Cox High school and others schools, was bringing in their students for a class. The students would have to order in Spanish from the menu the teacher would make, and I give them a special price. The Spanish teacher at Indian river HS also would order from me for her students Cuban Sandwiches. Pedro from the Recreation Center, also bought in the kids, I would give a small introduction of the kitchen and explain to them about Puerto Rican food.

It wasn't about the money it was about pride in my culture. I felt that Puerto Ricans were falling off the Latino map, because you would only here about Mexican food. People would come in asking for Mexican food so, I took that pretty hard. I marketed myself to everyone through the cuisine scene in the Virginia Pilot, the Echo, and the Tidewater Hispanic.

My son Andre wanted to get married to Jackie so I tried to price out a wedding. After looking at all the places which would cause me to close on a weekend, I decided to give him some money and do it at the Restaurant and invite the customers. My brother-in-law Pipo came over and rented a electric piano and played the music, plus I bought some big speakers and hooked up my computer to them and through windows media player we had music. It turned out great. I made a buffet of Puerto Rican food and pulled out some drinks and we had a wedding,

That was great Public Relations for the customers, and it cost me less than 200.00 dollars. I would close out 2004 with a bang! I didn't do my annual vacation. I opened for Christmas

Eve at night after I did my traditional dinner sales. I made a free buffet for military personal that were stuck here for Christmas in the area along with whoever wanted to come, but I would charge for the alcohol. We were packed and everybody who walked through the doors of Teresita's got a free plate of food plus a Home away from home atmosphere. I would also through a New Year eve party for who ever came through the doors it was free, but I would sell the alcohol, and soda, families came with their children, the children were outside running around, the parents were dancing and the salsa music blasting the sounds of our country, the restaurant was alive!! Puerto Ricans or Latino's had a place they could call their home, that was my whole dream and my wife especially, she who lived all her life in Puerto Rico, wanted to bring home to Virginia Beach. I also had her name in Light's; "TERESITAS" In lit up red letters. I guess I turned out to be a good husband after all. All thanks to God and My friend Leon, Ana, and my mother, and Father who taught me about community service.

My dad was the same way he never thought about himself his happiness was other people's happiness, and I got that from him, Eliacil Garcia RIP "dad I'm almost finished". I was generous because all that was giving to me came also from generosity, and I was making money and was very satisfied.

My son wanted to move out and get his new apartment and Jeanette also wanted to leave so they left and shared a 2 bedroom apartment across the street from the restaurant 1 room for Andre and Jackie, 1 for Jeanette. I then sold the house and picked up a nice chunk after the sale. I would pay off the Restaurants balance, that I did not pay before and the place was paid off. I moved into a new apartment to see what I wanted to do. My monthly personal bill all together was 1500.00 a month I had no car payments nothing just rent and utility bills plus I was getting extra money from Puerto Rico.

I was living pretty good, money in the bank. I was not bothered by the alcohol because I was still practicing the 12steps and working my spirituality, But I stopped writing in my journal, I would go months without writing so I was not watching myself and my connection with spirituality got a little weak, but I was fine, God have giving me all I wanted, however God also plays the stock market and expects a return on his investment. They started building town center and I secured a luxury apartment. I wouldn't move in till 8 months I wanted to live there, the restaurants they were building looked scary to a small family operation like mine, the big boys were taking over. I knew that it would hurt us a little. I was only 2 miles away.

I thought about getting a location there, but knew I would need at least 2million to be able to compete; I did not have that kind of money so I lowered my catering prices and started looking for more clients so I could at least stay afloat when the town center took off.

I catered to all The Tidewater Community colleges during Latin Month. I already had the Military, but every year they would come shorter and shorter. I decided to just let it go and keep cooking good food and not worry about them. My daughter was also bringing in a lot of customers, and we met our new daughter "Lilly" a country Girl from Puerto Rico who spoke no English and was very pretty and young. My wife liked her and so did I she would call my wife ma but she would call me, Tydie, she didn't know how to pronounce it. Jeanette would take her out and together they will spend their money at the mall buying clothes. My daughter ran around Va. Beach like a little queen she dressed great and people respected her, everybody knew me even the local bad guys, who would come in for food, they watch out for her at the clubs sometimes Jeanette would say "dad I can't meet nobody because of you "I said Jeanette honor that it's respect".

You also had Vinnie, Sharon, Jessie, Randi, Maria, Danny, Shelia, Leticia, Gilbert, old Gilbert, Milton, Arisol, Luz, Ralph, Neilsa, Susana, Debra, Gene, David, nick, Janet, Pedro, Eddie, Wanda, Tosco, Jose, Lee, Frankie RIP, plus many more. 2004-2005 were good years and I had everything working like clockwork. My Kids were independent Leonel, was living with us he was still a minor.

My renters were starting to come up short with the rent in December or 04, and I gave them a couple of months of free rent to get themselves together. I knew how it was so I try to help them, however they broke the lease and I let them out and thanked them for their time; after all they helped me get the loan by leasing the building. I would have to pay the mortgage, but was able to do it for 2005, for being a sport the old renters found me someone who was interested, so I decided to go to Puerto Rico for Christmas and meet the new renter and give him a lease.

Most of my regular's were going out of town so I gave everybody vacation after the party of the 24th that I would continue to do. So Jessie, and Danny, would go with me Jeanette, Leonell, and of course Teresita my wife to Puerto Rico. I rented an apartment and stood at ESJ towers in Isla Verde Puerto Rico. I met the new renter he paid me the rent for 2 months and asked me if I wanted to sell? I said we could talk about it later.

2006 would come in and I was thinking about buying a home my dream home where I would live to my final days on earth. I have decided to make Va. Beach my home for good. So I talked to Donald the mortgage man and he told me he could help me. I also decided to sell the property in Puerto Rico to the new Renter Taxes in Puerto Rico are brutal. I saw several houses but they were all high 400.000 and up, prices on houses were skyrocketing so I wanted to get me a house before the price got out of reach. I had sold my home in 05 for 199.000 which I paid 90.000, I said to myself if I get a 400.000 dollar house, I could sell it for 500.000 in 1 year if I struggle to pay. I mean everybody was buying overpriced houses appraised by the greedy banks, but I took my time and looked around Plus I was waiting for an answer from my guy In Puerto Rico. I got the call and he offered me a good price and I took it, so I started getting more serious about getting the house. I found a house in Courthouse Estates 4 bedrooms 2700 Square Feet, Jetted tub in the Master, lake in the back nice landscape, the living room wall had 3 large windows, and at night you could see the stars, Brick front, siding on the sides, the second floor had like a bridge and you could see the large windows, I mean It was a great looking house for me. I had the money to fill it with furniture. My wife loved it and so did I plus if my children ever needed to come back, I had a room for each of them. I gave Donald my information and he started to work towards getting me a loan, I said 2500 is my limit, he said "I could do better than that" I said great. I started looking at furniture, but something was telling me that I should really think about it. I thought God wanted me to have it! How ignorant I was. "God helps the needy not the greedy". God will help me, but he will not feed my ego. That house was all about ego 'I had leonell, me and my wife why did I need such a large house for? To show off?, The apartment in Town center was going to cost me 1600 a month. I was going to meet other potential clients for catering. I wasn't ready to take on the large Mortgage I was inheriting. The business was growing, but it needed room to breathe and I failed to take heed from the words of Leon, Short Solid Steps. I got lucky with Teresitas grill, but a 400.000 mortgage is no joke. I would become a victim of crises that would hurt the entire economy.

Chapter 11

In 2005 I would bring my Mother and father to Virginia Beach, my father was independent so I got them an apartment for people over the age of 55 it was pretty affordable for them. I would take them food from the restaurant whenever they wanted. My father would ride his motor scooter everywhere to the super market, Pharmacy, and he enjoyed riding his car. It was a lot better than Bronx River and cleaner air for them. In 2004 my mother had caught a stroke and was in a long term rehabilitation hospital, my father was getting tired of getting on the bus to go visit her every day. I started telling my dad that maybe it's time to leave and live in another place like Va. Beach. My dad thought about it and asks me to show him the area. A got him a plan ticket and flew to Virginia. I took my dad to see the apartment in Virginia Beach and he decided to move. And like my daughter, I took my parents out of 1440 Bronx River Ave also. It would be 50 years for them living in that neighborhood; my prayer was that they live in a house when in their last years. My dad always talked about planting tomatoes, and vegetables. I would work on that dream for them, but for now it would be an apartment. I got them set up with the local Doctors and took them to their appointments. I would take them out from time to time and my mother would love going to the restaurant to talk with people and she actually go into the kitchen and clean plates.

I would leave her alone, because she was feeling useful, my dad would always like to go home and watch TV that was his love. So I left him alone. My dad was a Yankees fan and Giants. I was very happy because, I was giving back to them and they were seeing their son success. The apartment was 5 minutes from the Restaurant.

In March of 2006 I moved into my New home in courthouse Estates and it was a dream come true, but I was worried of the mortgage I had to pay, $3400 a month mortgage, Leon must of rolled over in his grave on that one, that was too much, but I took the chance. I felt that if things got tuff I could sell it and turn a profit and buy a cheaper home; most of the country was thinking the same.

Teresitas Grill was doing well, and sales were up and would only drop a little, but the sales would go back up. I started including entertainment on Saturdays. I would get a guitar player and he would play some soft music till 9pm. Then a DJ would come and play till 2am, on Saturdays, I was the only Puerto Rican restaurant open at the time so the restaurant maintained itself full and the sales were great. People from as far as Washington DC were coming to my place; there was no Puerto Rican food nowhere In Virginia. I should have gotten some rich partners, because I could of put at least 5 more restaurants and never looked back. People from Northern Virginia would tell me that I needed to open up in that area, people from Ghent in Norfolk were begging me to put a Teresitas over there, but to do that you need partners with deep pockets and I didn't know anyone with that type of money.

I tried to play it safe and just stay with the one restaurant; my Roast Pork was the greatest. I remember a family of 4, dinninig 3 young daughters and their mother would come and order 4 roast pork dinners with rice and beans, an addition some plantains abd would leave there plates clean!

You go to all these beautiful Restaurants, and that's all they are beautiful the food is bland and you overpay for the ambiance, not what you went there for great tasting food. I'm talking about these huge restaurants with a million items on the menu and if you have any brains you must know a lot of those restaurants are just looks. I went to a lot of food shows and you can purchase precooked Hamburgers. In my Restaurant everything was made to order only the Roast Pork was cooked all night then all day for the evening crowd, and then placed in the steam Table, along with The Rice and Beans, Cooked daily. No one cooks better then a mom and pop restaurant.

I sold the building in 2006 and paid off the loan and Taxes, what was going to happen in the future, it would be the right thing to do sell.

The neighborhood was not good plus there were drug addicts in that area and there were a lot of robberies. So I had no interest in doing anything in that location. I put some money away and continued with my business. The new mortgage started digging into my savings. I started to worry, but had some good months and I would be stable again. I granted another wish! My mother in law once said that she wanted to see a show at Radio City Music Hall In Manhattan, so that Christmas I invited her to spend Christmas with us, she flew to New York. I got us 3 hotel rooms in Manhattan on 40th street, around the block from 5th avenue and tickets to see the Rockkett's a Christmas show at radio city music hall, that's the least I could do for the wife of a man who gave me the life I was having. I also invited the staff, eight of us would go.

We had to check out on the 30th of December, because that room I paid 125.00 dollars a night would become 900.00 a night for New Year eve. We went over to Jersey and found some cheaper prices and stood there for 3 more days. We had a great time and when we were at the show I saw Ana's face and she was happy. I love surprising people with their wish. A person should allow their thoughts to bring them what they want. Everything I've asked for I received, I wanted a family, received, I wanted a big house, received, I wanted to raise my daughter received, I wanted to find sobriety received, I wanted money received, a business received, bring my parents to live in Va. received, 2006 ended with much success. I couldn't wait for the next year which would put me 8 years in business.

I was catering to the local colleges and military and even the local people were calling me for catering, I also had a new catering contract with a Dominican lady called Judy, she would have me prepare lunch for local doctor offices so she could make presentation of new drugs in the market. All was working. Then the competition came in and I had 2 other restaurants surrounding me. I would have to share, which was ok, because I already had an 8 year head start. Unfortunately one of the restaurant owners husband was in the Navy so he had more access to the bases. I heard that some of the Navy people that were my customers were going over there along with some of my long time customers. Not to sound off on the other place, but I believed I had secured the loyalty from all the good things I did in the community, there were actually people happy to see me get competition, you know one thing I learned from the Chinese restaurant' there was one around the corner from me, but our back doors lead to the same area and when I try to talk to him he would brush me off with a stupid laugh, he was just here for business not friendship maybe that is why the Chinese are so successful.

Some of my long term customers started going to the other restaurant which is ok, but to be honest I was a little pissed. Though I did retain a nice amount of people that would keep me going and I would continue to build, but that 3400.00 dollar mortgage was starting to hurt plus the housing market was taking a turn for the worse and those high priced houses where unsellable. The pressure started to mount and I was getting a little wild in the kitchen.

My son Andre and his wife Jackie quit, because I was getting unbearable. What they didn't understand was I worried that we all be in the street. I would carry the burden of the problem myself my wife didn't even know half the problems we had. I started using my capitol reserves, because my sales dropped 50% over night and I would start to get behind. I would get mad because I took the money and property and put it all in Terisitas Latin Grill, in order to give my people something and also capitalize. They were not helping me. Some of my customers were feeling the same, but a large group of my customers were going to the other restaurant. People who when I visited Puerto Rico, I would go visit their family and share time with them, people who when a family member needed a job I would provide for them, people who when they needed a deal I would give it to them, yes those people. There were a few who was more dedicated to being my loyal friend and customer like Donald and his wife Leticia, Gilbert, Arisol, Milton, Ralph, Nilsa, Sheila, Luz, and her family also, and the rest of the crew. I would get over it and start to rebuild with new customers. I was getting more locals and we got back some customers that were just trying out the new cuisine at the other place. They would sit at the bar and tell me like it was ok to share with me that they went to the other place. "It sounds like this," . . . . hey honey . . . . I just had sex with our new next door neighbor! "But you're better" . . . . I know I sound like a crybaby, but when you see your life savings going down the drain it's very hard to sit there and be calm about your customers bailing out on you.

I guess my passion for my culture was wrong. The world is surrounded by envious people and success brings enemies. I would learn that the hard way in business. Andrew Carnegie was very generous, he was a philanthropist, but that was after he had become a billionaire. Business should stay business, till you close your doors, then you could do charity work, but not with your business, and definitely not in your beginning.

I should have learned from the Chinese owner. don't get close to your customers they are just customers, and they chase the price not the food, he didn't tell me that, It was Just by looking at his body language . . . It would cost me a half a million dollars, in order for me to learn that. Man I could have been a doctor with that money.

07 would end and 08 would come in and I would start to here the collectors call and the taxes mount up, fees, I was being buried in a mountain of fees. My account overdrawn and the ship would start to sink. I who thought highly of me started to lose everything, my daughter decided to go to New York because her mother got her into the Global Scholar Program, it was a full scholarship to guess where? Hostos Community College where I worked for so many years and was a bad drunk and addict. I was angry at my daughter, because I wanted her to study here in Virginia. She would walk the same hallways I walked at Hostoss Community College, but Tidewater Community College was not working for Jeanette. She saw how the bad times were starting to hurt me and she couldn't continue to watch. That would leave me with leonell, and terry, a young local Kid who also became like family, Terry was a white kid, I liked him a lot and me and my wife gave him the same love we give our kids, he learned also the menu and became a great sandwich and salad maker an addition to being a great kid.

I started getting behind on the house and the calls started, one day when I was at home alone I sat in my living room and shouted to God and said! "Why do you take away all that you have giving me" have I done something wrong? "All I do is give" I have been faithful to my wife and kids since day 1 why so many obstacles. I went into a crying frenzy, because I knew bad times were coming again. I had to prepare for the worse and I did. I confronted all the suppliers and tax people along with the landlord; I took all their criticism and would not allow my wife to hear any of it, like a real man I dealt with it. I tried to do whatever I can, but always came up short and would get beat up with fees. I started the process of getting out the house. I was giving a Foreclosure noticed and I told my wife, but it didn't bother her, she was by my side through the whole thing and never doubted me. We both would make a plan and I would assure her that I would not move her into a rattrap apartment. As the bills mounted and we couldn't pay anything, they cut of our gas at the house. Cold showers and no cooking, it was summer so it wasn't that bad. I would take the water hoses and bathe my wife with it because the water coming out the hoses was warmer. Here we are in this big house living like peasants. How low I felt for I failed as a man. I guess one does not have to be a drunk to fail in society.

I went bankrupt and found an apartment on Craigslist, on the Beach, Shore Drive an accountant who rents his Condo from August, to June. I took it and it was beautiful I lived on the 6th floor and had the view of the Chesapeake Bay Bridge 3 balconies and all the beach I wanted, I mean for a guy who just went bankrupt I look like I hit the lottery, my wife loved it and we would start on trying to fix our business. At night I would sit on the balcony and thank God for giving us such a nice place to live and also asked him to help me keep my business. I was very hurt and was very angry. I said to myself, why I didn't just stay In Puerto Rico when I got the Property, I could off done better. I had good relations with a bank and a paid off property "why, why, why, why, why did I stay in this fucking country that has done nothing but keep me down no matter what I do" . . . . I had an out and allowed myself to stay and fight for people who did not care. Does anybody have any pride, what did I do? The biggest hurt was they were my own people who let me down. The same thing happen to my father when he was doing well with the bus rides, the church group started doing it and eventually they were no more bus rides. We both looked out for our community. I guess it was part of my destiny.

I gave it a ride and took everybody with me, but the gas was running out. I would have to fight my way through everything I cannot believe how misfortune has followed me so much. I started to tell my wife get another husband, because I am bad luck. My wife throughout the whole ordeal was quiet and trusted in me. She never put me down or never lost her respect for me.

I would fight to win the battle, when she told me she loved me no matter what. I was willing to give my life in order for her and the kids to have all they wanted, you see my pride was my family not me. I wanted them to always have what they wanted and never cared about myself. I believe a man's job is to support his family and nothing else. Whenever we took vacation I would look at their faces and would feel great when they were smiling. Their happiness was my success. Well I had my work cut out for me and I was definitely ready to fight all the way to the end.

The final chapter 12

My wife and I started to clean up the mess. But we couldn't stop it, we kept sinking and sinking, and then the Government lends billions to the banks on Wall Street in order to stop a panic. The object was for them to lend money to people or businesses so the financial system could continue to be positive for the American people., The bank's did not lend anything at least to me they didn't. Small business would suffer in 2008; they were closing businesses left and right. I kept alive with the little I had left. The town center was booming and my Saturday nights were empty. I said "they would have to take me out of here in a coffin". I was not going out like the others. I remember one time the city tax officer came to get money from me and I didn't have any to give. I was getting behind own the meal taxes which is my responsibility to collect. My son Leo had 80 dollars in his wallet and gave it to the officer. The officer told me I needed to have the rest of the money on Monday. Which means I couldn't pay anything else, the City is strict on Meal Taxes and it's really not their fault, but here was the problem: A large of percentage of the sales was credit cards. When your bank account is steadily having multiple transactions being short isn't impossible. Since you needed to buy food to make money you would use it as soon as you got it. Your choices are very slim, and you have to manage with a microscope in order to stay afloat. But the landlord wants money, State, City, Feds, suppliers; it was hard to separate the taxes because of credit card sales, along with overdraft fees, because of others wanting to be paid in cash and me trying to pay everyone with the daily sales I was getting. A day came when I just wanted to scream, which I did. I walked into the walk in cooler then closed the door and just let out a large scream ahhhhhhhhhhhhhhhhhhhhhhhhhh!! Then went back to work, I felt like road kill and the vultures were just picking away.

The State was reasonable and would work with me, but they would kill you with fees. Here are the banks just giving billions of dollars from the Taxpayers and when I asked for help they would deny me and continue to kill my business with fees. I mean they even gave you fees on debit card transactions. Here is what they did,

Debit card transactions 100.00 balance, −$25.00, −$25.00, −$25.00, your balance should be $25.00 but here comes a check for −$100.00, they pay the check, but add 3—35 dollar fees for the debit card transaction an addition to the 75.00 dollars they had already approved. Your account than would look like this, −$185 instead of −$5 Then your sales were $375.00 but in the morning you have $190.00. Why not just return the check and hand me just 1—$35 fee. The reason for this is when you are falling the people start to own your thinking and logic, you become a lost soul in business and don't think, you are so beaten that you accept to give post dated checks that you know won't fly. It was a real madhouse, but I never gave up. I would program myself to just look at it as training.

When I had the bakery the first year and didn't accept credit cards I would at the end of the day pull out the taxes and save it. I would have no problem paying. Here I am today paying several hundred dollars a month in fees while the rich businesses are still making money and enjoying life. I am here broke living pay check to pay check because the government told me sorry we gave a supply of money to the banks why didn't you ask for a loan." Because you didn't regulate the loans 'jerk offs" The Wall Street bankers who saw doom saw paradise as they gave themselves bonuses, drove in limos, lived in mansions, and they told small business America go to hell. That my friends are the American Politicians we vote for, and the only capitalist are the Government and the Filthy Rich, the rest of us are just slaves.

A beacon score will tell the bank all about you. Imagine beacon scores in the 1890s and early 20th century? The ford Motor Company would have not existed, because Henry Ford failed several times before he found success. Many rich Americans always failed in the beginning, but they succeed once they have found the right formula.

Well another day would come and I found my wife in the back of the kitchen crying because the tax guy came, I usually deal with him, but he arrived before I can get there and he threatened to close down the restaurant. I begged him not to and I was given another chance to keep my doors open. I said it's not worth it, I guess I will lose. I put the restaurant up for sale. We started getting a lot of people interest in purchasing the restaurant, but none had any money, and I needed money because I owed taxes, rent, and some other bills. I would also need money to survive until I find a Job.

One night as I went home I bumped into the General sales Manager of Colonial Chevrolet, my old sales Job, I told him what had happen and he quickly told me He would welcome me back if I wanted the Job, I said thank you. I should have never left. If I would of stood at Colonial and never took this business. I would be sitting pretty Rich and maybe even a manager. One thing I did notice was Mike Really liked me as a salesman. We once would smoke cigars by the beach were we lived and talk. I was relieved, because now I have a job I could look forward to once I sell the restaurant and that took a lot of pressure of me. In December 2008, I was giving by Sheila a raffle ticket that would pay 1 million dollars if I won: it was the Virginia's New Years day Million dollar raffle. I said well maybe I win and pay off the bills and start all over again that would be a great gift.

There was a movie called "It's a wonderful Life" with Jimmy Stewart, the movie is about a business in financial trouble over a mistake, and of a rich man who took advantage of the mistake. He wanted to die because he couldn't face the realities that were ahead of him. An angel comes and helps him change his mind. In the end he runs in his house with happiness. A miracle took place, his clients had come back to repay him for all the good deeds he had done. They collected money and an old friend who was a successful businessman wired him some money, who ever made that movie had an imagination like mine; because when Sheila gave me that lottery ticket I believed the same fortune would come to me. I was already making plans. I believed. January 1st 2pm would come and I was already expecting the ticket to match the grand prize. I checked and I didn't win, but the ticket gave me the attitude I needed throughout the holidays. I called her and thanked her, but the sale would go on. I really enjoyed that ticket. I don't live in the realistic world. I live in a world of miracles and dreams. The realistic world is why people are always are depressed. I learned while a young lad in school that one must dream when in trouble with life situations though I knew my ride was coming to an end. I hit a milestone 10 years in business first Puerto Rican restaurant to last 10 years in Hampton Roads. I was looking for that woman who said that PR restaurants don't last in Hampton Roads 6 months; I would make her the fool for even saying that.

February came and I got a buyer Mr. T Latino the man with all the gold chains. We worked out a deal and I loved the idea of the restaurant staying Puerto Rican owned, If it wasn't going to be me at least let it be another Puerto Rican. He gave me a down payment and I paid the back rent and some taxes. On my last night of the Restaurant, I invited everybody and gave away food to those long loyal customers I had left, and as I sat in front of my computer playing music for my faithful friends, my tears started running down my face. I was hurt that it wasn't going to be me anymore. Some people would be happy they sold their misery. I felt as I was losing a child that I had raised and nothing could ever replace it. Nobody noticed it, but inside I was dying. I really loved what I did and I had allot of pride that I for so long kept rice and beans on the corner of Holland and south plaza trail. I had introduced Puerto Rican food to the locals. I won best of the beach, Puerto Rican food, was alive!! I help in the first 5 Latin festivals always with the long line and people faces full of happiness, and excitement. I also did a festival in Norfolk with Carlos, for 3 years anything that had to do with Puerto Ricans, or Latinos, Tyrone would be there even when I had no money I would find a way to help. At least I know one thing "I am Puertorriqueno De sangle y Corazon siempre". "My blood and Heart is Puerto Rican". I took of my chef jacket at 10.30 Pm and gave it to David and said don't let the restaurant fall, Never! I left and it was over, the date was March 15, 2009 exactly 10 years. Me and my wife left, and an era would die and be forgotten and a new one would start. We went to Puerto Rico and stood 2 weeks then came back and went to Disney world just me and my wife; she applied for a job at Amerigroup where she still is employed. I went to Colonial Chevrolet. I was not the same salesman, but sold a few cars and did 11 in one month, but the money wasn't the same and my attitude was terrible. I would quit and try something else it would go on like that for a couple of years. Once you are a boss in charge of your own it's hard to work for anybody. My sister would buy a house in Richmond Va. And she would take our parents, boy I lost everybody. My daughter was doing well she went to study for 3 weeks in Italy with her the Global Scholar group and 3 weeks in the Dominican Republic she got her Associates Degree and Invited me to her Graduation at Hostos Community College. The Honorable Sonia Sotomayor was the guest speaker and gave out the diplomas, plus Congressman Jose Serrano, Mayor Bloomberg, and Ruben Diaz. That was big and the people who still worked there from the days I was there remembered me and saw how I changed. They said that I looked good and they were happy to see me. I was very proud of my daughter. I guess she had to go there to tell the people what kind of a great dad I was, my ex wife Marisa works there and she eventually got her Master Degree, people said what a great Job I did with Jeanette, they told me how she was very smart, and always involved with all the clubs and has a great future. My other 2 boys were doing great Andres is doing great and married to Jackie working and living well. Leonell was going to TCC and is now at Norfolk State, he has a very nice Salvadorian Girlfriend called Sonia and I believe they will be Married soon. Sonia is a student at ODU and her family lives in Northern Va. We go up there once in a while to party with our new family and we are very excited about our future together. They are into the food and full catering business is something lurking here "I don't know, but God is very weird.

In 2011, I decided to go to Tidewater Community College. I did well my first semester and my writing was coming back to me. I always thought off writing a book, but felt I had no happy ending. So I have been waiting. Dr. Grant was my English teacher and all her assignments were essays it got me going, my other English class Prof. Sickles help me to find Information. Prof. Yandell taught me how to live and think as a college student in SDV, and my biggest fear Prof. Hamrick, algebra math, taught me how to solve problems. In January Of 2012, I would finally get a great job with Goodwill of Virginia thanks to the best manager at Goodwill TaNia, she hired me as an Assistant Manager paying me some decent money.

My 2nd semester of college is where I exploded in writing. I had Dr. Grant again Dr. Council in Public Speaking and I wanted to take a language. My Daughter suggested that I do, so she says daddy why don't you take French? I said "hell no" get me a Spanish class It should be very easy and I should be able to waltz through that class. Ha, Ha, Ha, Ha, well she looked up the Professors and I told her to find me a Spanish speaking Professor, Please! Because an American accent will throw me off and it wasn't going to sound right. Well she says I don't see anyone, but here is one that has my name spelled with a G which means she has to be great dad, I said ok sign me up instead of Jeanette it was Prof. Ginette Eldredge. I said different. Well I started classes and was very excited about the Public Speaking, and my very easy Spanish class.

My Spanish class was first so I go to class, not knowing that this class would change my entire life. I walk into the class and meet the Professor and noticed she looked Latina, I said well I guess I got what I wanted to learn Spanish from a Latino/ Latina Professor. The moment she started talking I knew she was Puerto Rican. I know Puerto Rican woman very Good. I also knew she was from the Island; I was very happy inside that finally in all my life I had a teacher that was Puerto Rican. I felt as it would be an adventure and the rest of the class was pretty cool, unfortunately I was terrible. I was so lost in Spanish; this is not so easy. I would pass the first test, but by test 3 I was swimming with the sharks. I had scored a 69. Though I wasn't studying the way I should I felt as I could just figure it out? The Professor was very good she taught with a lot of passion and you could tell she loved her culture and was very consistent, but what ignited me was One time as I emailed her for help. I saw a Poem written on the bottom of her E-mail It was in Spanish it was a poem written by a 16th century play writer and poet called Calderon De la Barca, who also wrote a play for King Henry the eighth and would become a priest at 50 years old. It was a poem of dreams and since I was a dreamer who always took unrealistic chances it motivated me to write some of my life stories in Spanish. There the title "Soap that doesn't clean" which in Spanish is "El jabon que no limpiar" an essay I wrote was born. I started to write about my thoughts and part of my life in Spanish. I would show the Professor and she would correct it for me. It helped me more in the class. It started to bring back parts of my life and my mind was becoming a Television set again like in rehab.

I just started jotting down Information. I would start this book but in a different way. I felt that all my failures were nothing, but stories and that within I was a writer and I needed to write this book. I always talked about writing one, but sometimes God puts people in your life to give you a push and it was Prof. Ginette Alomar. Eldredge that did it, along with a poet from the 16th century. I wasn't going to write this far, but every night I sit outside and look at the stars I felt like I should take the story all the way to the month of May when I actually started putting my writings into Chapters. I started writing on May 14th its know June 14th going into June 15th 1 am in the morning. My mother is dying and we expect to hear the news any day, so before I go into mourning, I want to finish. My Dad died last year on March 17 2011, my next goal after this book is to write short stories in Spanish. However I still have several semesters of Spanish left.

I would love to see Puerto Rico change and start using the fields full of plantains and vegetations, and capitalize. I would love to see the crime in Puerto Rico go away, and Jobs to go up, I would love to see Puerto Rico run its country a lot better, I would love to see Puerto Rico get back all the educated Puerto Ricans on the mainland and go back and rebuilt its corrupt Government, I would love to see the United States stop using Puerto Rico like it's mistress and fully commit, or let us build our own country, I would like to see all those other Latino Immigrants who use our island to get to New York respect and honor our Island and stop talking bad about us when you reach NY, or try swimming to the shores of The U.S. There is still time to save the Island right now crime controls more than democracy. Dr. Pedro albizuu Campos saw all of this coming 100 years later we are still fighting poverty, corruption, crime, and now drugs, I want to be part of that group that help's fix the island. If we are going to be American well dam it lets do it and start to capitalize and stop being puppets to the Americans! let's be equal. America it's time Puerto Ricans on the Island vote for the President, because if we can't then give me my independence, And take all the Puerto Ricans that don't want to stay and build with you. We can all be friends, we can all be allies, we could all be part of the human race, but I don't want to be your puppet any longer.

The semester went well and I eventually passed all my classes 2 A and 1B the B was in The Spanish class. Spanish is a beautiful language not an easy one neither, I saw myself writing very dramatic in it and that is why I love it so much.

My mother Died On Tuesday June 19th 2012 at 7pm she was able to see me sober for 22 years which is a great accomplishment. I love America, America is a beautiful country it's just a few bad apples that destroy what everybody else is trying to build, peace and prosperity for all, however I also love Puerto Rico and I demand respect from this day on. In the words Of Dr Pedro Albizu Campos "when tyranny is law revolution is order" and that goes for the Island. And can The New York Jets finally win me and the fans a Super Bowl. You could do It Rex. I want to end this book with this; I am light, I am human, and I am love, I love everybody, even the ones that hurt me including my first grade teacher who humiliated me. I also have come to the understanding that soap cannot clean who you are! We are all different in color, but the same within and must accept that. We all suffer the same way, die the same way, and get sick the same way, let's stop the ignorance and start to grow. I would find out later that my first grade teacher was put in a mental Institution, no wonder I lived such a crazy life my first teacher was nuts. I would also go to the nut house for alcohol and Drug abuse, but the most important of all that with all the obstacles I had to fight, especially during sobriety, not once, did the thought of drinking alcohol cross my mind, that is how powerful the 12 steps of recovery are if you practiced correctly. God will help you! He won't help your Ego, and to tell you the poem I read on the Email, here it goes in English and in Spanish it would be the last words of Segismundo Soliloquy.

What is life? A frenzy. What is life? An illusion, a shadow, a fiction, and the greatest good is small, that all life is a dream, dreams are dreams".

¿Qué es la vida? un frenesí. ¿Qué es la vida? una ilusión, una sombra, una ficción; y el mayor bien es pequeño; que toda la vida es sueño, y los sueños, sueños son" . . . Calderon de la Barca

amen

Acknowledgements

Professor Ginnete A, Eldredge, and Dr. Gloria Grant for the awakening, the poet who is been deceased for maybe 400 years Calderon De La Barca, Jenifer Wilson, Who gave me the thumbs up on the book. I also want to thank Goodwill of Virginia for given me a Job: for if I didn't have this job I couldn't pay for the services I needed to write this book. I also want to throw out a big hug to the best crew in the entire world, The Dam Neck Crew Goodwill store 141. Theresa, Kim, Ms, Inez, Holly, Glenda, Janelle, Jessita, James, Jenifer, Melanie, My original crew. Danielle, Mike, Robert, Zack, Doris, Cat, You will all be successful. The one and only biggest helper of all! "The Powers of the Universe God almighty", for without that power I am worthless.